INSIDE HEAVEN AND HELL

What History, Theology and the
Mystics Tell Us about the Afterlife

THOMAS W. PETRISKO

INSIDE HEAVEN AND HELL

*What History, Theology and the
Mystics Tell Us about the Afterlife*

—————

THOMAS W. PETRISKO

St. Andrew's Productions

iv

CONSECRATION
AND DEDICATION

This book is consecrated to the Most Holy Trinity and is dedicated to my confessor, Rev. Joseph P. Newell. May God reward him abundantly for his steady, fearless preaching of the Gospel.

St. Andrew's Productions
6111 Steubenville Pike
McKees Rocks, PA 15136

Copyright © 2000 by Dr. Thomas W. Petrisko
All Rights Reserved

Second Printing, *2001*
Third Printing, *2002*

ISBN 1-891903-23-3

Phone: (412) 787-9735
Fax: (412) 787-5204
Web: www.SaintAndrew.com

Scriptural quotations are take from The Holy Bible —RSV: Catholic Edition. Alternate translations from the Latin Vulgate Bible (Douay Rheims Version —DV) are indicated when used. Some of the Scriptural quotations from the New American Bible: St. Joseph Edition, The New American Bible— Fireside Family Edition 1984-1985, The Holy Bible—Douay Rheims Edition, The New American Bible — Red Letter Edition 1986.

PRINTED IN THE UNITED STATES OF AMERICA

ACKNOWLEDGMENTS

I wish to thank those most helpful to me during the writing of this book: Dr. Frank Novasack, Fr. Richard Whetstone, Fr. Bill McCarthy, Michael Fontecchio, Amanda DeFazio, Carole McElwain, and the prayer group at the Pittsburgh Center for Peace.

I thank my family for the support and sacrifice they have made for this work, my wife Emily, daughters Maria, Sarah, Natasha, Dominique and my sons, Joshua and Jesse. As always, a special thank you to my mother and father, Andrew and Mary Petrisko and my uncle, Sam.

ABOUT THE AUTHOR

D r. Thomas W. Petrisko was the President of the *Pittsburgh Center for Peace* from 1990 to 1998 and he served as the editor of the Center's nine special edition *Queen of Peace* newspapers. These papers, primarily featuring the apparitions and revelations of the Virgin Mary, were published in many millions throughout the world.

Dr. Petrisko is the author of seventeen books, including: ***The Fatima Prophecies, At the Doorstep of the World; The Face of the Father,*** *An Exclusive interview with Barbara Centilli Concerning Her Revelations and Visions of God the Father;* ***Glory to the Father,*** *A Look at the Mystical Life of Georgette Faniel;* ***For the Soul of the Family;*** *The Story of the Apparitions of the Virgin Mary to Estela Ruiz,* ***The Sorrow, the Sacrifice and the Triumph;*** *The Visions, Apparitions and Prophecies of Christina Gallagher,* ***Call of the Ages, The Prophecy of Daniel, In God's Hands,*** *The Miraculous Story of Little Audrey Santo,* ***Mother of The Secret, False Prophets of Today, St. Joseph and the Triumph of the Saints, The Last Crusade, The Kingdom of Our Father, Inside Heaven and Hell*** *and* ***Inside Purgatory*** *and* ***Fatima's Third Secret Explained.***

The decree of the **Congregation for the Propagation of the Faith** (AAS 58, 1186 - approved by Pope Paul VI on 14 October 1966) requires that the *Nihil Obstat* and *Imprimatur* are no longer required for publications that deal with private revelations, apparitions, prophecies, miracles, etc., provided that nothing is said in contradiction of faith and morals.

The author hereby affirms his unconditional submission to whatever final judgment is delivered by the Church regarding some of the events currently under investigation in this book.

TABLE OF CONTENTS

ARE YOU GOING TO HEAVEN?

Fr. Bill McCarthy, MSA

Are You Going to Heaven? That is, are you going to spend your eternity with God? This is perhaps the most serious question that anyone has to deal with or answer. One time, one of the disciples asked Jesus, "Lord, are they few in number who are to be saved?" Now that is a very interesting question. In short, Lord when all is said is done, will most people go to Heaven or Hell?

Listen to the answer that Jesus gives. I guarantee you, it may shake you up a bit. He meant it to shake us up. Or, even better, He meant it to shake us down, that is to shake all sin out of us. Listen very carefully to His answer. He replied, "Try to come in through the narrow door. Many, I tell you will try to enter and be unable. When once the master of the house has risen to lock the door, and you stand outside knocking and saying, 'Sir, open the door for us,' he will say in reply, 'I do not know where you come from.' Then, you will begin to say, 'We ate and drank in your company, you taught in our streets.' But he will answer, 'I do not know where you come from. Away from me you evildoers,'" (Lk 13:22-27). In the Gospel of Matthew, Jesus gave the same teaching. But He put it a little differently. "Enter through the narrow gate, the gate that leads to damnation is wide, the road is clear, and many choose to travel it. But how narrow is the gate that leads to life, how rough the road, and how few there are who find it!" (Mt 7:13-14).

The words of Jesus could scarcely be clearer. The road to salvation is narrow, not wide. And few, not many, find it. How it must have cost Jesus to answer that question so clearly. After all He said and did, Jesus full well realized that most people would reject him and His cross and prefer to live in mortal sin and thus lose their souls. In a sense, the teaching of Jesus was not new. The prophets of the Old Testament consistently warned the Israelites that only a remnant would in fact respond to God in such a measure as to share in His salvation. Isaiah foretold, "A remnant will return, the remnant of Jacob to the mighty God. For though your people O Israel, were like the sand of the sea, only a remnant of them will return; their destruction is decreed as overwhelming justice demands," (Is 10:21-22. Cf also Jeremiah 23:3ff, Micah 2:12; and Zachariah 8:12).

Once again Thomas Petrisko has written a gem — a challenging and provocative book on the highest good — God and Heaven. He sets aside naive notions and grounds us in the splendor of the truth that God wishes to share His own Divine Life with us eternally. There is a Heaven. It is a narrow road there. Jesus is the way. Yet the Father is most merciful. Are you going there? Dr. Petrisko knows the way and shows the way. This book is MUST reading, especially for lent when we get more serious about the state of our souls. Excellently researched, well documented, inspirationally written!

– Fr. Bill McCarthy, M.S.A.
Moodus, CT
February 7, 2000

INTRODUCTION

IS THERE AN AFTERLIFE?

"Repent! For the Kingdom of Heaven is at hand." These words, Christ's very first in public, not only revealed the design of His mission but shaped the question of who is worthy of this Kingdom. Although we can't be certain of how this initial pronouncement was received 2,000 years ago, the lively response to Pope John Paul's 1999 discourse on Heaven may be a clue to what theologians say has always been, and remains to this day, a controversial part of the faith.

"Heaven has many cartographers, and through the centuries many different heavens have been charted," wrote Howard Chu-Eoan in a 1997 *Time magazine* cover story on today's varied perceptions of Heaven. In this article Chu-Eoan focused on why American religion has distanced itself from salvation's reward, making Heaven seem like a paradise lost. But though diverse opinions on the afterlife exist, such diversity does not mean that people lack belief. To the contrary, a *Time/CNN* poll conducted in 1997 found that 81% of Americans believe in Heaven and that 61% feel that it is where a person goes immediately after death. While only 1% of Americans feel that a soul can go directly to Hell, Heaven, it seems, still maintains enduring appeal for Americans from one end of the denominational spectrum to the other.

"Eye has not seen, ear has not heard… what God has ready for those who love Him" (1 Cor 2:9). These words from Scripture, perhaps more than any other, inspire us to delve into the mystery of Heaven, a mystery many of the faithful today seem confused or uncertain about.

From a Christian perspective, Holy Scripture seems to

guarantee that a life of faith will result in a great, eternal reward. We expect this reward—Heaven—to truly possess the beauty, wonder, glory, magnificence, and awe depicted so loftily in traditional Judeo-Christian writings. But in a skeptical world, how can we still believe in what some people consider an anachronistic concept?

We've all heard the latest theories about Heaven: Heaven is within us; Heaven is an idea; Heaven is an attitude; Heaven is not a real place—everyone goes to Heaven! While these concepts are theologically shallow, many people adhere to these new perceptions of Heaven, despite what the Church teaches.

But what is the truth? Is Heaven a place? Is it a condition? Or is it both? And if we believe in Heaven, what about the souls who managed to get there? Were they rewarded for perseverance in their earthly trials? Or did reunion with God require goodness and faith?

And what about the souls who do not go to Heaven? Do they go to Purgatory? Or Hell? Didn't Christ emphasize that the road to Heaven is narrow? Indeed, while there may be pearly gates and ecstatic joys, this celestial city certainly sounds as if it's also a walled fortress, something else many people today absolutely refuse to believe.

In a series of audiences (Summer 1999) on the afterlife specifically designed to call attention on the eve of the Great Jubilee to what should be the most important part of every Christian's life— one's eternal destination of Heaven or Hell— Pope John Paul II stirred the international media with talk of the definitive existence of Heaven, Hell and Purgatory.

While the discourses primarily stressed the "conditions" of such afterlife states verses their "places", the mere subject of the "afterlife" quickly caught the wind and provoked a number of articles that, more than anything else, revealed the great debate that still exists over the existence, makeup, conditions and locations of Heaven, Hell and Purgatory.

Heaven, the Holy Father stressed, was "the ultimate end and fulfillment" of the deepest human longings, "the state of supreme, definitive happiness."

On the other hand, Hell was, the Pope said, the state of those who "freely and definitively separate themselves" from God. "Damnation", said John Paul II, was the state "freely chosen by the human person and confirmed with death that seals this choice forever."

God's judgement, he added, "ratifies this state."

Purgatory, the Pope explained, is "a condition of being open to God, but still imperfectly." It is a condition where "every attachment to evil must be eliminated, every imperfection of the soul corrected. Purification must be complete, and indeed, that is precisely what is meant by the Church's teaching on Purgatory."

★

While the Pope's teachings were certainly intended to stir the faithful in a positive way in regards to their march through life towards the Kingdom of God, both here and after, the three discourses were unfortunately manipulated by popular media reports to something more than the Pope intended them to be. With his preference of emphasis on the conditions of the afterlife realms, Pope John Paul II obviously hoped his listeners would understand how God's love and mercy are at the center of these teachings. And in living one's life, one's decisions were already shaping their eternal realities, their eternal "conditions" of either bliss or woe.

However, from this emphasis came quickly the effort by some to imply that the long held belief in "places" of afterlife did not exist and that the Church was now teaching something new. The media reports included isolated quotes by certain theologians and hierarchy that lent more "spin" to the impression that the Pope was all for the modern picture of life after death. Heaven and Hell were not places of celestial merriment or eternal fire, the articles emphasized, but rather states of "mental being" either in communion with God or not. There was especially a strong effort to minimalize the truths of Purgatory and Hell. Purgatory was "a condition of life," not a place at all, and Hell was "everlasting frustration" not eternal fire. And moreover, the media suggested that prior teachings had been symbolism and today's understanding now evolved well beyond such nonsense.

★

While the Pope indeed spoke of the necessity of realizing the presence of symbolic language in the New Testament, it must be noted that his teachings were not intended to establish any new theological understanding of the afterlife. Indeed, the Church has always emphasized the "nature" of the state of the beatific vision (Heaven) and that of the principal pain of Hell — separation from God.

However, beginning with the Fathers of the Church, Tradition has always held and does to this day that such an understanding would be incomplete with out the recognition of the places of the afterlife. Indeed, many Doctors, Popes and Saints of the Church have written of the "places" of Heaven, Hell and Purgatory and to this day, these places (as well as conditions) have been defined and upheld by theologians of every generation.

Moreover, there is no reason to believe that the Pope meant anything new by his teachings. While the exact location of these abodes remains unknown, the fact that the Church teaches the just and the unjust will have resurrected bodies clearly implies, as it always has — that these bodies (reunited with their souls) will dwell in specific locations. As the Catholic Encyclopedia states about Hell, "hence we may say Hell is a definite place; but where it is we do not know." Likewise, many Catholic writers have traditionally emphasized that both Jesus and Mary are in Heaven in body and soul already, once more implying that the place of Heaven is a true place not within the earth, but beyond.

Thus, it is clearly Catholic Tradition that it is not enough to say that souls exist in just the state of a condition after death and not in a place. There must be, the faith demands, the undertaking of the existence of a place, although we know not where. Wrote Frank Morris in the Wanderer edition of September 16, 1999: "It is accepted teaching that the resurrected do not have a different kind of body, but the very body of that earthly life (Council of Toledo) — and bodies (unlike spirits) must exist at or in a place. Indeed, it is the presence of matter that "makes" place. Place may be defined as the locus of bodies."

The teaching of this reality has not been confined to Tradition. Private revelation is rich with visions, dreams, and precise accounts from visionaries and chosen souls who have spoken to Mary, Jesus or an angel about the afterlife worlds of Heaven, Hell and Purgatory. At Fatima, Portugal, where the Virgin Mary's apparitions to three children occurred in 1917 and were later fully approved by the Church in 1930, the children described a vision of Hell so detailed with information concerning the conditions and place of Hell, so graphic in its overall revelation of this horrifying abode, that it was beyond question something, Church scholars have said, they could not have made up.

Similarly comes today the accounts of the afterlife from many visionaries, especially the seers at Medjugorje.

★

This book opens no new understandings of the afterlife. It does, however, uphold what Christians, and especially Catholics, have always been taught concerning Heaven, Hell and Purgatory: the conditions and abodes of these afterlife states are real and they await each and every soul.

While some may not like what they are about to read concerning the full nature of these revealed states, I can only prayerfully suggest that they investigate for themselves, before endangering their souls to contemporary concepts of the afterlife that feel good but defy thousands of years of God's revelations, that which Judeo–Christian literature has long held to be the truth.

Our Father in Heaven awaits the return of all His children to Himself. May this book, in some little way, contribute to His great longing.

Michelangelo's rendition of '*The Last Judgment*' was painted on the wall of the Sistine Chapel in Rome.

CHAPTER ONE

LOOKING FOR HEAVEN

B elief in a blissful afterlife for the just did not originate in Holy Scripture. Long before Christianity, long before the prophets of Israel voiced a progressive revelation regarding the remuneration of the just after death, the concept of an afterlife was found in ancient civilizations. Anthropologists note that as far back as the Stone Age, prehistoric people buried their dead in the hope that there was life after death.

The earliest grave yet to be discovered was found inside a limestone cave north of Peking, China, near a village named Choukoutien. In this 400,000 year-old cave, anthropologists believe they've found evidence for deliberate burial practices that involved a hope in a spiritual world. Thousands of years later, the Neanderthals practiced similar burial ceremonies. While excavating a cave near Shanidar in the remote Zagros Mountains of northeastern Iraq, bodies were discovered in graves that contained flowers. The flowers suggest that the Neanderthals had hope in an afterlife of beauty and happiness. Through discoveries of ancient artwork, poetry, narratives, theology, architectural remnants, and folklore, various concepts of belief in an afterlife are discernible in almost every prehistoric civilization.

Over time, ancient cultures developed more profound concepts of life after death, concepts that nurtured hope in a place of eternal "peace" and even eternal "pleasure." These beliefs involved a heavenly place that was a continuation of life on earth. Some beliefs even began to integrate human experiences, such as the principle of vindication through divine justice. This vindication was viewed as necessary for one to enter Heaven and revealed how good and evil were thought to be present not only in this world but in the next.

Approximately 5,000 years ago, Egyptian burial practices exhibited a conscious awareness of this concept. Scholars say amulets concealed in a person's death wrappings were intended to guard the soul from evil spirits on its journey to Heaven. After 3100 BC, during the reign of the Pharaohs, Egyptian burial rituals evolved into a cult of the dead, as the devout rigorously prepared for an eternal destination of peace, a "paradise of the spirits."

During this era, anthropologists say the Sumerians of the ancient city of Ur, the reputed birthplace of Abraham, also became involved in an afterlife cult that prepared the dead for eternal life. This preparation included religious practices for the living to prepare them for their heavenly destination. Temples were built for their gods, and complex ceremonial rites were used to bury their priests and priestesses. Similar practices and preparations are found in the remnants of ancient cultures throughout Africa and Asia and with the early inhabitants of the Americas.

Several thousand years later, early Persian teachings on the afterlife—which some writers suggest influenced the development of later Jewish beliefs about Heaven—also focused on a doctrine of resurrection. This doctrine involved a future life in Heaven or Hell and belief in a cosmic battle between good and evil.

The concept of a bodily resurrection first appeared in the teachings of the Persian prophet Zoroaster, a Babylonian king and prophet who is reputed by some historians to have lived around 2400 BC, though most historians place him later. Zoroaster taught that a person's fate after death depended on an individual judgement of his/her earthly life. This judgment resulted in either reward in Heaven or condemnation in Hell. Complete happiness would occur when the soul was finally reunited with its earthly body. Zoroaster foretold of a general resurrection of the dead, a messiah, a universal divine judgement, and a purification of the earth which would restore it to its original perfection and beauty. In this new world, Zoroaster prophesied that people would live forever.

By the time early Judaism emerged, the ancient Near East was a melting pot of diverse peoples who, although we know little of them, shared similarities in culture, language, and religious beliefs. During the 18th century, scholars created the word "Semitic" to describe this group of people who were primarily Assyrians, Babylonians, Canaanites, Persians, Phoenicians, and Hebrews.

The world, according to Semite belief, was a three-tiered house containing an upper realm of Heaven where the gods dwelled, a middle human world governed by the gods, and a lower netherworld where the dead and infernal deities dwelled. Semites believed the upper world and lower world influenced human life and that communication with these worlds was of great importance. Therefore, regardless of one's station in life, the gods of both worlds were needed because peace depended on their graciousness. Eventually, the Semite religion developed into a complicated belief system of ritual and lore. Ancestor worship and priestly skills were essential in securing the powers of Heaven and the Netherworld. Public liturgies and private rituals were celebrated by individuals, families, and communities with the intent of receiving desired blessings.

In the Semite religion, the dead of both the upper and lower worlds retained their form, consciousness, and memory. They also had knowledge of what was happening in the middle world. The dead had the power to harm or to aid the living and such power affected every element of life. Holy Scripture offers a glimpse of Semite beliefs in the story of King Saul who, in desperation, turned to a seer for help. Colleen McDannell and Bernhard Lang revisit the story in their 1988 book *Heaven, A History*:

> The living contacted the dead not only through ancestor worship but also through mediums and wizards who had access to the netherworld. In one necromantic session described in the Bible, King Saul attempts to learn the outcome of an imminent battle. Finding that his normal channels of communication with the divine realm—dreams, priestly manipulation of lots, the advice of prophets—have failed, he turns to other means. Out of desperation Saul resorts to a necromancer. In a night-time consultation, Saul's medium digs a hole in the crust of the earth so that the world of the living may be joined to the realm of the dead. Eventually the witch announces that a deceased prophet has ascended for questioning. Only she can see

the "old man, wrapped in a robe," and only she can
actually communicate with the spirit and pass on the
messages received. The consultation ends with the
spirit's clear announcement that Saul will lose his life in
battle the very next day. The dead expect him soon in
the other world. Then the fading spirit returns to the
darkness and silence of Sheol. Saul, of course, dies as
foretold during the consultation.

The Semite concept of a spiritual dimension reveals the
expanding development of belief systems in an afterlife. But it is in the
Greek and Jewish histories that we find the full emergence of a theology
of Heaven.

Historians tell us that both ancient peoples started out imagining
a gray, undifferentiated afterlife called *Hades* by the Greeks and *Sheol* by
the Jews. But in Greece, the great philosophers slowly began to
confront the pagan belief of where the honored dead went and to
challenge the location of their two mythical, afterlife sites—the Isles of
the Blessed and, later, the Elysian Fields. Supposedly, after death the
souls of the virtuous were transported to the *Islands of the Blessed*, or the
Happy Islands. These islands were located westward in the ocean at the
end of the earth.

In classical Greek mythology, *Elysium* was also a place where
souls of the just went after death. There are three conceptions of
Elysium found in Greek writings. First, Elysium is revealed in Homer's
Odyssey to be a place located westward in the ocean at the end of the
earth where specially favored mortals were transported by the gods to
enjoy perpetual blessedness. This relocation was believed to occur
without separating the soul from the body. Secondly, Pindar and
Hesiod identify Elysium with the Islands of the Blessed, claiming that
it is situated on these same islands. Thirdly, a concept which appeared
much later and is the least common appears in Virgil's *Aeneid*. Here
Elysium is part of the lower world in which the souls or "shades" of the
good dwell.

In Greece, the early, unsophisticated pagan teachings of Hades
did not last. The Greek philosopher Aristotle declared that all
polytheistic religious needed to unite in placing the home of gods in the
most elevated regions of the universe. Such places were considered

closed to ordinary mortals. The Islands of the Blessed, Aristotle argued, were reached only by heroes and the favorites of the gods. Eventually, corresponding to the Greek philosopher's theology, there emerged in Greece a belief in a timeless, spaceless realm of pure spirit and mind. Unlike the earthly netherworlds of the Isles of the Blessed, souls in this realm had perfect knowledge of eternal essences. In contrast, other polytheistic religions conceived of Heaven as a place where mortals might continue to enjoy earthly pleasures. Examples of this would be the German and Scandinavian Valhalla and the Native American Happy Hunting Grounds.

Similar to what the Jews would eventually believe, the Greeks emphasized the image of Heaven as being in the sky, a holy firmament stretching across the stellar spheres where God and His beloved creatures were reunited and existed as in a community. In the Greco-Roman religion, the afterlife became a happier place as belief grew that heroes — so virtuous and noble and certainly loved by God — would be destined for a better life after death. The blessed were believed to ascend into the sky, leaving earth behind, and especially Hades — the place of punishment.

The Pythagoreans, around 600 BC, were the first Greek philosophers to advance the doctrine of immortality in Heaven and the transmigration of souls. The philosopher Parmenides described Heaven as timeless, eternal, indestructible, invisible, and unchangeable. He also perceived it as being beyond human passions and in need of nothing.

Plato conceived that a human being's spirit was essentially linked to the spiritual world. He determined that the location of the Isles of the Blessed was in a heaven above the stars. Plato, who also moved the location of the Elysian Fields skyward, reasoned that the soul contained the most vital aspects of the person. He believed that once the soul was released from the body, the spirit became stronger and more powerful. It was then refined and became god-like and so ascended upward to Heaven. Plato championed the concept of judgement after death in his *Gorgias*. In *Phaedo* he forwarded the belief that the human soul should strive upward after its death. Plato also believed that the life force in all living things (*psyche*) and the mind (*novs*) constituted the "soul" and that the soul was immortal because of its affinity for the divine.

Five centuries after Plato, the Neoplatonists formed a religious system based on Plato's philosophy. Plotinus, Proclus, and others insisted that everything in the cosmos, through love, yearned for the divine. Cicero, a Roman philosopher, lawyer, and politician also carried on Plato's ideas in promoting the concept of reward and punishment in another life. Later, Philo of Alexandria, a Jewish-Hellenistic philosopher born in the 1st century BC, wrote that the soul joins in Heaven the incorporeal inhabitants of the divine world—the angels. Some souls, Philo suggested, ascended even higher to live with deity.

Belief in a heaven developed even before Divine Revelation because the history of Heaven is really the history of human hope. From the earliest times, humanity has longed and hoped for Heaven. Over time, through reason, the Greeks developed not only a concept of law, but a new concept of God and Heaven. This concept of God offered man such hope that even Socrates embraced it. And his subsequent refusal to believe in the "gods of the state" resulted in his eventual execution.

Perhaps most importantly, Plato asked the very profound question of whether "a holy thing is holy because the gods approve it, or do the gods approve it because it is holy?" This question refers to what might be considered "divine essence." The Greeks attempted to understand the "essence of Heaven" through contemplation of "eternal truth." Although this Greek concept of Heaven sprang from the human heart, which always seeks goodness and truth, it was developed and refined through human reason.

However, the Hebrew concept of Heaven came not from human reasoning but from God. It was born of the hope found in the soul, not in the mind. This concept differed from all previous concepts of Heaven in that it was God-given. Through it the Jews offered mankind a revelation of Heaven that resonated not only in the human mind, but in the heart and soul of man. Heaven, the Jews insisted, was not just for heroes, but for everyone—for they believed that everyone was a "child of God." This revolutionary idea was, for the Jews, the purpose for heaven. For them, it was God's home—a place where He would be reunited with his earthly children.

CHAPTER TWO

THE PROMISED LAND

C hristians believe that God ordained Old Testament events to foreshadow later events in Christ's life. This foreshadowing is especially evidenced in the Hebrew desire and search for a promised land, a presage of what should be every Christian's ultimate goal—Heaven.

Indeed, the wisdom of learning to understand the greater picture from an earlier, lesser one marks to a degree the impetus behind all foreshadowing acts of God. But in the case of Heaven, it must be acknowledged that God didn't deny His chosen people, the Jews, the reality that they too should set their eyes on something above and beyond the land of milk and honey. Heaven, God's abode, was a house with rooms to be filled and the God of Abraham, Isaac, and Jacob let this be known to the Jews.

But unlike the Greek Heaven which was revealed by man and based on human philosophical truths, the Hebrews attributed their conception of Heaven to God. They insisted that they were only messengers chosen by the one, true God to reveal Himself and His Kingdom to His people. Peter Kreeft, a philosopher and author, defines the difference between the Heaven of the Greeks and the Heaven of the Jews:

> If a visitor from another planet had observed the face of the earth some twenty-five centuries ago with an eye sensitive not merely to external but also to internal energies, he would have singled out not Persia or Egypt but Greece and Israel as the waves of the future and the

roots of history's civilized tree. They were the only two peoples who found modes of thought other than myth for answering life's three great questions. For myth the Jews substituted faith in a historically active and word-revealing God, and the Greeks substituted critical, inquiring reason. For this reason they developed different hopes, different heavens, from those of the myths.

The Hebrew conception of heaven arises in exactly the opposite way from the pagan one; instead of rising out of humanity's heart, it descends from God's as the New Jerusalem descends out of the heavens at the end of the story in Revelation. From the beginning of the story, God tells humanity what he wants instead of humanity telling God what it wants. Instead of humanity making the gods in its image, God makes humanity in his image; and instead of earth making heaven in its image, heaven makes earth in its image. Thus the greatest Jew teaches us to pray: "Thy Kingdom come ... on earth as it is in heaven."

The good Jew therefore does not speculate about heaven. If it has not entered into "the heart of man," well then, whatever *has* entered into "the heart of man" is not it. Let God define it and provide it, not humanity. Only when God speaks do we know with certainty, and when God speaks obscurely, we know only obscurely. Jews, unlike Christians, do not believe God has spoken clearly about the afterlife (at least not yet), and they will not run ahead of God—a proper and admirable restraint when contrasted with the extravagant myths of the rest of the world, who succumb to the irresistible temptation to fill in with human imagination the gaps left in God's revelation.

The Greeks are the other root of the tree of Western civilization. The Jews gave us conscience; the Greeks, reason. The Jews gave us the laws of morality, of what ought to be; the Greeks gave us the laws of thought and of being, of what is. And their philosophers discovered a new concept of God and a new concept of heaven. While the priests were repeating their stories of fickle and fallible gods with their Olympian shenanigans and imaginative afterworlds, underworlds, or overworlds, the philosophers substituted impersonal but perfect essences for the personal but imperfect gods and a heaven of absolute Truth and Goodness for one of pleasures or pains. Not Zeus but Justice, not Aphrodite but Beauty, not Apollo but Truth were the true gods: perfect unpersons rather than imperfect persons. (The Jews, meanwhile, were worshiping a Perfect Person, transcending the Greek alternatives.) The heaven corresponding to the Greek philosopher's theology was a timeless, spaceless realm of pure spirit, pure mind, pure knowledge of eternal essences instead of the priests' gloomy underworlds of Tartarus and Hades, earthly otherworlds of Elysian Fields, astronomical overworlds of heroes turned into constellations....

Goodness and Truth, stand above the Greek gods. But they do not stand above the Jewish God, the God who *is* Goodness and Truth, *emeth*, fidelity, trustworthiness. The Greeks discovered two divine attributes; the Jews were discovered by the God who has them.

Like the Greeks, the early Jews' hope in an afterlife was rooted in the belief of a shadowy, gray, undifferentiated place called Sheol. Like the Greek underworld of Hades, Sheol was where the souls of the dead descended after leaving their bodies. The Jews believed Sheol to be a neutral place of neither pain nor pleasure. This belief was adopted, more or less, from the Semites who also believed in Sheol and a benevolent deity named Mot who ruled there. But we quickly find a progressive revelation of the afterlife in the Old Testament of the Jews.

In Genesis we read that after his death, Abraham "was gathered to his people." The Lord is called "the God of Abraham, the God of Isaac and the God of Jacob." Yahweh is said to "bringeth down to hell and bringeth back again," that "he killeth and makes alive again," and that after his death, Moses, like Abraham, was "gathered to his people."

As time moved on, the great Jewish prophets also spoke of the recompense reserved for the just after death. In Isaiah, we read of "The new heavens and the new earth... a rejoicing, and the people thereof, joy." These passages point to the obvious: the God of the Jews dwells above in a special abode and He is reserving it for the arrival of His chosen people.

While the Jewish conception of Heaven in Scripture is quite different from the Christian, it is the same in one critical way: it is offered not as inspired writing but direct revelation of truth from God. Thus, references to an afterlife with God are seen as God's way of providing a basis of faith for His chosen people. This faith was institutionalized through the Covenant that was handed down from Adam to David. And it provided those who were faithful to God with the hopeful belief that they would be rewarded for their faith—in this life and in the next. Scriptural experts date this Jewish idea of reward after death from the time of the Babylonian captivity. This period in Jewish history was rich in prophetic writings which shifted the focus of Jewish hope from blessedness on earth to blessedness in the next world, the life of the hereafter.

According to scholars, the perception of Sheol slowly began to change. One portion of Sheol was associated with Gehenna, a fiery abode where the unfaithful perpetually burned after death. A second part of Sheol was understand as a shadowy abode for the mediocre. Finally, a third part was designated as a place of comfort and rest for those that deserved it. These concepts were modified as the prophets began to reveal that the just deserved a much better fate than the unjust and a new eschatological promise of transformation surfaced: "For I am about to create new heavens and a new earth; the former things shall not be remembered or come to mind. But be glad and rejoice forever in what I am creating, for I am about to create Jerusalem as a joy and its people as a delight" (Is 65:17-18).

As more such writings emerged, Sheol was reduced from three parts to two—Sheol was below the earth and Heaven was above. A resurrection of the body and soul began to emerge in Holy Scripture, as did the notion of eternal life—an eternal life with God in Heaven filled with joy, praise, and celebration.

The Book of Daniel, according to Jeffery Burton Russell in his *History of Heaven*, contains the first clear reference to resurrection in

Jewish thought: "At the end of the world those who sleep in the dust of the earth shall awake, some to everlasting life, and some to shame and everlasting contempt" (Dan 12:2). Ezekiel, a prophet alive during the Babylonian Exile, also transmitted a series of hope-filled oracles in such an afterlife. These included visions of a gloriously rebuilt Jerusalem.

In one vision, Ezekiel is shown a plain strewn with human bones. He is then commanded to prophesy to the bones, announcing their transformation and resurrection. In the vision, the bodies are re-formed and God orders Ezekiel to breathe on them to restore life. This Scriptural passage is, for many theologians, the foundation for Jewish belief in Heaven.

By the 1st century BC, the Pharisees taught that the body would rise from the dead in glory to be with God forever. The Pharisees affirmed this belief at the Council of Jamnia in 90 BC, and it remains an orthodox Jewish belief to this day.

Images of life eternal are woven into the verses of the Old Testament, as is symbolism and apocalyptic accounts of a celestial paradise and the coming of a Messiah. Clearly, the theological truth of Heaven as the abode of God is defined and maintained: "Look down from Heaven and regard us from your holy and glorious palace. Where is your zealous care and your might. Your surge of pity and your mercy? O Lord, hold not back" (Is 63:15). Other references from the Old Testament establish and develop this truth as well:

- **HEAVEN IS EVERLASTING:** "One generation passeth away and another generation cometh, but the earth abideth forever" (Eccles 1:4).
- **GOD CREATED HEAVEN:** "In the beginning God created the heaven and the earth" (Gen 1:1-2).
- **THERE WILL BE REWARD IN HEAVEN FOR THE JUST:** "Behold the Lord hath proclaimed unto the end of the world, say ye to the daughter of Zion, Behold thy salvation cometh, behold his reward is with him, and his work before him. And they shall call them, the Holy people, The redeemed of the Lord: and thou shalt be called, sought out, a city not forsaken" (Is 62:11-12). "We shall be filled with good things of thy house" (Ps 61:5).

- **HEAVEN IS A PLACE:** "I saw heaven open" (Ezek 1:1). "Open ye the gates, and let the just nation, that keepeth the truth, enter in" (Is 26:2). "Thou shalt no more have the sun for thy light by day, neither shall the brightness of the moon enlighten thee: but the Lord shall be unto thee for an everlasting light, and thy God for thy glory. Thy sun shall go down no more, and thy moon shall not decrease: for the Lord shall be unto thee for an everlasting light, and the days of thy mourning shall be ended. And thy people shall be all just, they shall inherit the land for ever, the branch of my planting, the work of my hand to glorify me" (Is 9:19-21). "O Israel, how great is the house of God, and how vast is the place of his possession! It is great, and hath no end: it is high and immense" (Bar 3: 24-25).

- **HEAVEN IS A PLACE OF HAPPINESS:** "Thou hast made known to me the ways of life, thou shalt fill me with thy countenance: at thy right hand are delights even to the end" (Ps 15:11). "They shall be inebriated with the plenty of thy house; and thou shalt make them drink of the torrent of thy pleasure. For with thee is the fountain of life and in thy light, we shall see light" (Ps 35: 9-10). "Glorious things are said of thee, O city of God. The dwelling in thee is, as it were of all rejoicing" (Ps 96: 3). "He shall cast death down headlong for ever: and the Lord God shall wipe away tears from every face, and the reproach of his people he shall take away from off the whole earth: for the Lord hath spoken it. And they shall say in that day: Lo, this is our God, we have waited for him, and he will save us: this is the Lord, we have waited patiently for him, we shall rejoice and be joyful in his salvation" (Is 25:8). "And in that day the deaf shall hear the words of the book, and out darkness and obscurity the eyes of the blind they shall see. And the meek shall increase their joy in the Lord, and the poor men rejoice in the Holy One of Israel" (Is 29:18-19). "Then shall the eyes of the blind be opened, and the ears of the deaf shall be unstopped. Then shall the lame man leap as a hare, and the tongue of the dumb shall be free; for waters are broken out in the desert, and streams in the wilderness. And a path and a way shall be there and it shall be called the holy way; the unclean shall not pass over it, and this shall be unto you a straight way, so that fools, so that fools shall not err therein. No lion shall be there, nor shall any mischievous beast go up by it, nor be found there: but they shall walk there and shall be delivered. And the redeemed of the Lord shall return and shall come into Sion with praise and everlasting joy shall be upon there heads; they shall obtain joy and gladness, and sorrow and mourning shall flee away"(Is 35:5; 68:10). "For behold I create new heavens, and a new earth: and the former things shall not be in remembrance, and they shall not come upon the heart. But you shall be glad and rejoice in these things which I create: for behold I create Jerusalem a rejoicing, and the people thereof joy. And I will rejoice in Jerusalem, and joy in my people, and the voice of weeping shall no more be heard in her, nor the voice of crying" (Is 65:17–19.)

- **HEAVEN IS A PLACE OF REST:** "There the wicked cease from tumult, and there the wearied in strength are at rest. And they sometime bound together without disquiet, have not heard the voice of the oppressor. The small and great are there, and the servant is free from his master" (Jb 3:17–19).

- **HEAVEN IS ETERNAL:** "Let nothing hinder thee from praying always, and be not afraid to be justified even to death: for the reward of God continueth for ever. (Eccles 27:22). God will clothe thee with the double garment of justice, and will set a crown on thy head of everlasting honor" (Bar 5:2).

- **HEAVEN IS THE OBJECT OF OUR HOPE, THE DESIRE OF THE HEART:** "As the heart panteth after the fountains of water; so my soul panteth after thee, O God. My soul hath thirsted after the strong living God; when shall I come and appear before the face

of God?" (Ps 12: 2-3). "For I know that my Redeemer
liveth and in the last day I shall rise out of the earth. And
I shall be clothed again with my skin, and in my flesh I
shall see my God. Whom I myself shall see, and my eyes
shall behold, and not another: this my hope is laid up in
my bosom." (Job 19: 25-27). "I believe to see the good
things of the Lord in the land of the living" (Ps 26:13)

- **HEAVEN MUST BE EARNED:** "The life of man
  upon earth is a warfare, and his days are like the days of
  a hireling" (Job 7:11).

It is important to point out that the Jewish revelation of Heaven
differs from the later Christian revelation. Russell notes that while the
ideas of resurrection and immorality in Heaven are shared to a degree,
the Jews believed that at the moment of death the faithful Jew either
enters a final state of blessedness or awaits reunion with the body and
then enters the new Jerusalem. For Jews, the place of resurrection is to
be the Mount of Olives and all who rise will be judged.

Although early Jewish teaching instructed that the righteous
either entered the new Jerusalem or Paradise, later Jewish teaching
eventually allowed for man's entry into Heaven, which had previously
been thought to be only for God. The Jewish Heaven, according to
Russell, integrated agriculture, pastoral, and urban elements: "On the
banks on both sides of the river will grow all kinds of trees with food.
Their leaves will not wither nor their fruit fail but they will bear fresh
fruit every month, because the water for them flows from the sanctuary.
Their fruit will be for food, and their leaves for healing" (Ezek 47:12).
Russell also adds that for the Jews, Heaven is not just a place: "The
heavenly Jerusalem is a glorified time as well as place; it is the Day of the
Lord, the Day of Judgement and reward; it is the Festival Day, it is the
Day of rest, the eternal Shabbat, the sabbath of sabbaths, *"shabbath
shabbathon."*

In the Jewish Heaven, the dead dwell with God. But Russell
points out there is little support in the Hebrew Scriptures for the
Christian belief that the saved will see God:

Between the Lord and the cosmos that he created a great
gap is fixed; Judaism is the exact opposite of pantheism.

Yet God, though wholly distinct from the cosmos he has made, dwells in it through his Shekinah (his presence throughout his creation, his light and his glory). Jacob and Moses both see God, but God tells Moses: "You cannot see my face; for no one shall see me and live.....While my glory passes by I will put you in a cleft of the rock, and I will cover you with my hand until I have passed by; then I will take away my hand, and you shall see my back; but my face you shall not see" (Ex 33:20-23). We can see the Shekinah, or what the Christians would call a theophany or action (*energeia*) of God, but we cannot see his face, his essence, his Being (*ousia*).

Not long before the Christian era, Jewish literature entered what is known as the "apocalyptic period." The writings of this era included Old Testament Apocrypha and the pseudopegrapha (writings falsely attributed to honored early figures, such as some of the patriarchs and prophets). Neither Jewish or Christian literature ever accepted these writings, but they contained a number of different themes concerning Heaven. Visions, dreams, and prophecies were included in the alleged revelations of divine secrets—past, present and future. And again, the resurrection, last judgement, and many metaphorical accounts are used to describe Heaven.

These included the number of heavens, the secrets of Enoch, divine sights, the saints, and the music of Heaven. The rejected texts even described what is said to surround God (glory, purity, light, power, and impenetrable brightness), although His face remained concealed. For the most part, rabbis generally dismissed such apocalyptic literature. On the whole, they believed Heaven would be reconstructed on earth, the resurrection of the body and judgement would take place in the geographical Jerusalem at the end of time, and that there the Kingdom of God would reign.

During the pre-Christian period and after the first century of Christianity, the Jews continued to examine their own ideas about the afterlife. Far from being static, the topic of Heaven remained a serious subject, but one also constantly affected by individual, family, and national concerns, as well different interpretations of theological concepts.

Religious movements, destruction of the Second Temple, and the demise of ancient Israel also influenced the Jews' understanding of God, Who He was, where He was, and what exactly occurred in life after death. But the basic tenets of Heaven remained firmly rooted for the Jews. And this proved to be fertile ground for the greater revelation of God's Kingdom which would eventually come through the life and death of a Jew—Jesus Christ.

Chapter Three

INHERITING THE KINGDOM

Although early Christians embraced the basic tenets of a Jewish Heaven, Christ provided them with a full revelation through His life and words. He explained that Heaven was not only a place where God lived, but a special sanctuary prepared for His children: "Come ye blessed of my Father. Inherit the kingdom prepared for you from the creation of the world" (Mt 25:34).

With pronouncements such as this, Christ described Heaven as God wanted it to be known. And frequently he compared it to a kingdom, one ruled by a king in truth and justice. One in which the subjects gave praise and glory to their king, not out of fear, but to love and honor Him: "It will go well with those servants the master finds wide-awake on his return. I tell you, he will put on an apron, seat them at the table, and proceed to wait on them" (Lk 12:37).

Scriptural scholars say the Gospels do not say much about the "place" of Heaven, but what is revealed is enough to establish a concise and clear doctrine of Heaven. Heaven, Christ said, is a vast, permanent abode created from the beginning with its subjects' arrival in mind: "In my Father's house there are many dwelling places: otherwise how could I have told you that I was going to prepare a place for you? I am indeed, going to prepare a place for you, and then I shall come back to take you with me, that where I am you also may be. You know the way that leads where I go" (Jn 14:2-4).

A belief that both the Jews and Christ shared was that Heaven was for the blessed (Mt 25:34), and that in order to enter into eternal life, it was necessary for man to keep God's Commandments. Admittance was granted to each person based upon his/her earthly existence: "If you wish to enter into life, keep the commandments" (Mt 19:17).

But besides the promise of justice in Heaven, Christ also promised that Heaven was well worth the discipline and obedience needed. He viewed it as a priceless possession: "The kingdom of heaven is like a merchant's search for fine pearls. When he found one really valuable pearl, he went back and put up for sale all that he had and bought it" (Mt 13:45-46). Christ emphasized that Heaven was nothing like this world: "My Kingdom does not belong to this world....my Kingdom is not here" (Jn 18:36).

In the beginning of Matthew's Gospel, Christ challenges mankind to "Reform your lives, The Kingdom of heaven is at hand" (Mt 4:17). For He had come to help fill Heaven with souls— obedient souls of faith. In speaking of obedience, Christ was referring to God's Law: "Do not think that I have come to abolish the law and the prophets. I have come, not to abolish them, but to fulfill them. Of this much I assure you, until heaven and earth pass away, not the smallest letter of the law, not the smallest part of a letter, shall be done away with until it comes true. That is why whoever breaks the least significant of these commands and teaches others to do so shall be called least in the kingdom of God. Whoever fulfills and teaches these commands shall be great in the kingdom of God. I tell you, unless your holiness surpasses that of the scribes and Pharisees you shall not enter the kingdom of God" (Mt 5:17-20).

Christ also emphasized the connection between Heaven and "holiness." Throughout the Gospels, He pointed out that Heaven's best example of holiness was God the Father. Repeatedly, Christ associated God the Father with the Kingdom of Heaven, even calling the Father His "Heavenly Father." The Father is perfect, said Christ, and, therefore, future inhabitants of Heaven must seek perfection, too. So from directing prayer to our Father "who art in Heaven" to following the Father's example in seeking holiness, Christ was teaching that the Kingdom of Heaven was intended to be filled with "holy" souls—souls who were aligned with our Father's Divine Will. He cautioned that this path was a narrow one and that "few" find it on their own.

However, the Gospels reveal that the very purpose of Christ's coming was to help offset this difficulty. Christ, therefore, is to be understood as the way, the truth, and the life: "Whoever acknowledges me before men I will acknowledge before my Father in heaven.

Whoever disowns me before men I will disown before my Father in heaven" (Mt 10:32-33). Indeed, the most "perfect" path to Heaven's gate is a life lived in union with Christ, for Christ is the doorkeeper to the Kingdom: "Father, Lord of heaven and earth, to you I offer praise, for what you have hidden from the learned and the clever you have revealed to the merest children. Father it is true, you have graciously willed it so. Everything has been given over to me by my Father. No one knows the Son but the Father, and no one knows the Father but the Son—and anyone to whom the Son wishes to reveal Him" (Mt 11:27).

As with the Greek, Jewish, Semite, and even Persian concepts of Heaven, Christ reaffirmed the inevitable judgement of the soul. However, the Christian view of judgement would not be solely based on a person's actions, as believed by earlier religions, but even on words and thoughts. This was a new and much broader teaching: "I assure you, on judgement day people will be held accountable for every unguarded word they speak. By your words you will be acquitted and by your words you will be condemned" (Mt 12:37).

Although the path to Heaven was narrow and difficult, Christ was sent by our Father to guide us there. And to provide the children of God with His ongoing presence and support, Christ established His eternal Church. He said to His apostle Peter that "I for my part declare you are 'Rock' and on this rock I will build My Church and the jaws of death shall not prevail against it. I will entrust to you the keys of the Kingdom of heaven. Whatever you declare bound on earth, shall be bound in heaven, whatever you declare loosed on earth shall be loosed in heaven" (Mt 16:18-19).

During His ministry, Christ revealed much about Heaven. The Gospel of Matthew is especially rich with the Lord's teachings on Heaven:

- **DENIAL OF SELF:** "Whoever would save His life will lose it, but whoever loses his life for my sake will find it. What profit would a man show if he were to gain the whole world and destroy himself in the process. What can a man offer in exchange for His self" (Mt 16:25-26).
- **EARNING HEAVENLY MERIT:** "The son of Man will come with His Father's glory accompanied by

His angels. When he does he will repay each man according to his conduct" (Mt 16:27).

- **THE NEED FOR CHILDLIKE VIRTUE TO GAIN HEAVEN:** "I assure you, unless you change and become like little children, you will not enter the kingdom of God. Whoever makes Himself lowly, becoming like this child, is of great importance in the heavenly reign" (Mt 18:3-4).

- **THE NEED FOR PURITY:** "If your eye is your downfall, gouge it out and cast it from you. Better to enter life with one eye than be thrown with both into fiery Gehenna" (Mt 18:9).

- **THE NEED FOR FORGIVENESS:** "My heavenly Father will treat you in exactly the same way unless each of you forgives his brother from His heart" (Mt 18:35).

- **THE NEED FOR KEEPING THE COMMANDMENTS:** "If you wish to enter into life, keep the Commandments" (Mt 19:16).

- **THE DANGERS OF THE TRAPPINGS OF MATERIALISM:** "I assure you, only with difficulty will a rich man enter the Kingdom of God" (M t 19:23).

- **THE REWARD IN HEAVEN FOR SACRIFICE:** "Everyone who has given up home, brothers or sisters, father or mother, wife or children or property for my sake will receive many times as much and inherit everlasting life" (Mt 19:29). "Anyone among you who aspires greatness must serve the rest" (Mt 20:26).

- **THE ABSENCE OF MARRIAGE IN HEAVEN:** "When people rise from the dead, they neither marry nor are given in marriage but live like angels in heaven" (Mt 22:30).

- **THE RESURRECTION OF THE DEAD:** "As to the fact that the dead are raised, have you not read what God said to you, I am the God of Abraham, the God of Isaac, the God of Jacob? He is the God of the living, not the dead" (Mt 22:32).

- **THE VALUE OF PERSEVERANCE IN GETTING TO HEAVEN**: "The man who holds out to the end, however, is the one who will see salvation" (Mt 24:13).

- **THE FACT THAT CHRIST HIMSELF WOULD CONDUCT THE LAST JUDGEMENT AND ISSUE A VERDICT**: "When the Son of Man comes in his glory escorted by all the angles of heaven, he will sit upon his royal throne, and all the nations will be assembled before him. Then he will separate them into two groups, as a shepherd separates sheep from goats. The sheep he will place on his right hand, the goats on his left. The king will say to those on his right, 'Come. You have my Father's blessing! Inherit the kingdom prepared for you from the creation of the world. For I was hungry and you gave me food I was thirsty and you gave me drink. I was a stranger and you welcomed me, naked you clothed me, I was ill and you comforted me, in prison and you came to visit me.' Then the just will ask him: 'Lord, when did we see you hungry and feed you or see you thirsty and give you drink? When did we welcome away from home or clothe you in your nakedness? When did we visit you when you were ill or in prison? The king will answer them: 'I assure you, as often as you did it for one of my least brothers, you did it for me.'

Then he will say to those on his left: 'Out of my sight you condemned, into that everlasting fire prepared for the devil and his angels! I was hungry and you gave me no food, I was thirsty and you gave me no drink. I was away from home and you gave me no welcome, naked and you did not come to comfort me. Then they in turn will ask: "Lord, when did we see you hungry or thirsty or away from home or naked or ill or in prison and not attend you in your needs. He will answer them: 'I assure you, as often as you neglected to do it to one of these least ones, you neglected to do it to me.' These will go off to eternal punishment and the just to eternal life" (Mt 25:31–46).

In Mark, Luke, and John's Gospels, Christ clearly lays out the path to Heaven. Through His parables and teachings, He emphasizes the definitive existence of Heaven. Faith in Him and obedience to the Commandments are again the key. In addition, a soul must hunger for Heaven now—in this life. Again, Mark's Gospel, like Matthew's, illustrates how sacrifice and renunciation of worldly things leads to eternal life and how Christ would, through the sacrifice of His life, open the gates of Heaven—even to the Gentiles.

In the Gospel of Luke, optimism prevails. Christ has come to extend an invitation to Heaven for all mankind. He describes Heaven as a celestial community with saints such as Elijah and Moses. And He clearly distinguished between the earthly and heavenly Paradise. Christ explained that while the earthly paradise, or Eden, existed at the beginnings of creation, the heavenly paradise, or New Jerusalem, would exist at the end of the world..

In John's Gospel, more than the Synoptic Gospels, Christ's divinity is central to His teachings on Heaven. Heaven, therefore, becomes not just a place of material reward but of the ultimate reward: union and participation in the divine—especially in the Father. Moreover, Christ reveals in John how in coming down from Heaven, He became the bread of life—eternal life, and, therefore, the Eucharistic Sacrament He institutes, a Sacrament from Heaven, is the surest way to reach Heaven. The full Gospel teaching of this mystery and how it relates to Heaven is worth reviewing:

> Jesus said to them, "I am the bread if life; whoever comes to me will never hunger, and whoever believes in me will never thirst. But as I told you although you have seen [me], you do not believe. Everything that the Father gives me will come to me, and I will not reject anyone who comes to me, because I came down from heaven not to do my own will but the will of the one who sent me, that I should not lose anything of what he gave me, but that I should raise it [on] the last day. For this is the will of my Father, that

everyone who sees the Son and believes in him may have eternal life, and I shall raise him [on] the last day."

The Jews murmured about him because he said, "I am the bread that came down from heaven," and they said, "Is this not Jesus, the son of Joseph? Do we not know his father and mother. Then how can he say, 'I have come down from heaven'?" Jesus answered and said to them, "Stop murmuring among yourselves. No one can come to me unless the Father who sent me draws him, and I will raise him on the last day. It is written in the prophets: 'They shall all be taught by God.'

Everyone who listens to my Father and learns from him comes to me. Not hat anyone has seen the Father except the one who is from God; he has seen the Father. Amen, amen, I say to you, whoever believes has eternal life. I am the bread of life. Your ancestors ate the manna in the desert, but they died. I am the living bread that came down from heaven; whoever eats this bread will live forever; and the bread that I will give is my flesh for the life of the world." (Jn 6:35–51)

Again in the Gospel of John, as in the synoptic Gospels, Christ warned that Heaven cannot be reached but through Him:

He said to them again, "I am going away and you will look for me, but you will die in your sin. Where I am going you cannot come." So the Jews said, "He is not going to kill himself, is he, because he said, 'Where I am going you cannot come'"? He said to them, "You belong to what is below, I belong to what is above. You belong to this world. That is why I told you that you will die in your sins. For if you do not believe that I AM, you will die in your sins." (Jn 8:21–24)

Christ used the analogy of a sheepfold and sheepgate to explain his role and purpose as mankind's shepherd:

"Truly I assure you: Whoever does not enter the sheepfold through the gate but climbs in some other way is a thief and a marauder. The one who enters through the gate is shepherd of the sheep; the keeper opens the gate for him. The sheep hear this voice as he calls his own by name and leads them out. When he has brought out [all] those that are his, he walks in front of them, and the sheep follow him because they recognize his voice. They will not follow a stranger; such a one they will flee, because they do not recognize a stranger's voice." (Jn 10: 1-5)

Even though Jesus used this teaching figuratively with them, they did not grasp what He was trying to tell them. He therefore said [to them again]:

"My solemn word is this: I am the sheepgate. All who came before me were thieves and marauders whom the sheep did not heed. I am the gate. Whoever enters through me will be safe. He will go in and out and find pasture." (Jn 10:1-9)

Again in John's Gospel, Christ depicted Heaven as having "many mansions," and that desire for Heaven was a worthy desire, for it is indestructible and everlasting. "Labor not for the meat which perisheth but for that which endureth unto life everlasting" (Jn 6:27).

The Gospels may reveal little about the "place" of Heaven but much about what a soul can expect to feel or experience there: love, peace, joy, security, and, most importantly, the beatific vision of God. Heaven, then, is not so much material pleasure as an eternal communion with God. It is, therefore, more than a reward. It is a home—a home for those who have arrived through love of God, having followed in Christ's footsteps.

CHAPTER FOUR

THE NEW JERUSALEM

Nothing is more pleasing to the eye than light. Thus, if the Gospels shed a new spiritual light on Heaven, the same must be said about the Epistles. At the core of these writings are the words of St. Paul, who confidently speaks of visions of Heaven and the truths of Heaven's splendor. His words, powerful and provocative, reveal that his experiences with Heaven surpasses all the ear could hear, the eye could see, and the heart could desire. And repeatedly he emphasizes Christ's promise of personal reward for each soul in Heaven: "Every man shall receive his own reward, according to his own labor" (1 Cor: 3-8), and "He who sows sparingly will reap sparingly, and he who sows bountifully will reap bountifully" (2 Cor: 9-6).

St. Paul's writings on Heaven clarified that the Messiah's Kingdom was not earthly or material. Rather, it was a spiritual kingdom. His Epistles refer frequently to the "resurrected body," reminding us that contemplation of Heaven should be "spiritual," not earthly.

In Heaven, said Paul, the elect will see God face to face (1 Cor: 13-12) and, he emphasizes in his First Epistle to the Thessalonians, that to be in Heaven is to be with Christ: "for where Christ is there is life, the kingdom of life" (1 Thess: 4-17). Moreover, this eternal union in Christ is what caused Paul to write what is perhaps the ultimate depiction of the coming glories of Heaven: "Eye has not seen, ear has not heard, nor has it dawned on man what God has prepared for those who love him" (1 Cor: 2-9).

For his own part, St. Paul declared that he had actually been to

Heaven, and that while there, he had heard language which he was unable to verbalize: "I must go on boasting however useless it may be, and speak of visions and revelations of the Lord. I know a man in Christ, who, fourteen years ago, whether he was in or outside his body, I cannot say, only God can say—a man who was snatched up to the third heaven. I know that this man, whether in or outside his body, I do not know—God knows—was snatched up to Paradise to hear words which cannot be uttered, words which no man can speak" (2 Cor: 12-1-4).

St. John's writings were equally meaningful in expanding the Christian concept of Heaven. In St. John's *Letters* and his *Book of Revelation*, the Evangelist concurs with St. Paul—that those in heaven would see the face of God (1 Jn:3-12; Rev 22:4). This was critical, for at that time, Jewish theology contradicted this teaching. Heaven, John revealed, was not only radically different from this life, but in keeping with Christ's and St. Paul's teachings, was primarily "union with God." It was a reunion of God with His children.

The *Book of Revelation* graphically depicts mankind's journey to Heaven, individually and collectively, as a war between the Celestial Court and the legions of Satan, a universal battle between good and evil—combat between the power of light and the force of darkness. These insights about Heaven are based on St. John's visions of angels, heavenly creatures, glorious lights, God's throne, and other celestial wonders. His divinely inspired depiction of mankind's salvation history concludes with the coming of the "New Jerusalem." St. John saw that this full coming of the Kingdom of Heaven at the end of time would transform our earthly world, a world deeply wounded by evil—especially idolatry, apostasy, and violence.

St. John's Heaven specifically refers to a renewed world in Christ. Clothed in symbolism, his *Book of Revelation* advances the imagery of Heaven far beyond anything previously revealed. While seen by scholars as having its roots in the writings of Ezekiel, Daniel, and other Old Testament apocalyptic writers, St. John's radical new revelation broadened mankind's understanding of Heaven. Jeffery Burton Russell writes of this in his book, *A History of Heaven*:

> The *Apocalypse* [*The Book of Revelation*] reveals
> that the world is soon to be renewed. The divine figure
> on the throne says he is "making all things new" (Rev

21:5). "Then I saw a new heaven and a new earth; for the first heaven and the first earth had passed away.... And I saw the holy city, the new Jerusalem, coming down out of heaven from God, prepared as a bride adorned for her husband" (Rev 21:1-2). It is renewed and completed. The figure on the throne says, "It is finished! I am the Alpha and the Omega" (Rv 21:6).....

The New Jerusalem was described as being filled with the glory of God and a radiance like a very rare jewel, like jasper, clear as crystal. It has a great, high wall with twelve gates, and at the gates twelve angels, and on the gates are inscribed the names of the twelve tribes of the Israelites.... And the wall of the city has twelve foundations, and on them are the twelve names of the twelve apostles of the Lamb.
The angel who talked to [St. John] had a measuring rod of gold to measure the city and its gates and walls. The city lies foursquare, its length the same as its width: and he measured the city with his rod, fifteen hundred miles; its length and width and height are equal. (Rv 21:11-16)

The shape of the heavenly city is modeled on the Ark of the Covenant, the Temple, and the Temple Square (Ezek 45,48; 1 Kings 6). The New Jerusalem is a sacred space whose boundaries are the boundaries of creation itself, for what is outside it is not anywhere at all.

John's heaven, unlike that of the Jewish pseudepigrapha, lacks a temple. "I saw no temple in the city, for its temple is the Lord God Almighty and the Lamb" (Rv 21:22). The wall of the city "is built of jasper, while the city is pure gold, clear as glass. The foundations of the wall of the city are adorned with every jewel.... And the twelve gates are twelve pearls, each of the gates is a single pearl, and the street of the city is pure gold, transparent as glass" (Rv 21:19-21). The "four-horned golden altar before God" (Rv 9:13) corresponds to the one that stood in the Tabernacle and the Temple in the holy place of Israel (Ex 27). At the

center of the heavenly city is the garden where God sits
on his throne. Temple, throne, and garden bring
together the images of heaven as tabernacle, city, and
paradise. "Then the angel showed me the river of the
water of life, bright through the middle of the street of
the city. On either side of the river is the tree of life with
its twelve kinds of fruit, producing its fruit each month;
and the leaves of the tree are for the healing of the
nations" (Rv 22:1-2). The waters of life flow from the
source of life and light, while the waters under the earth,
which represents chaos, formlessness, and death, vanish
or are purified into a clear sea of glass or crystal before the
throne. The leaves and the fruit offer healing and
wholesome nourishment.

God on his throne is the true king of Israel, the
king of all nations, king of all the cosmos. "Then I saw
a great white throne and the one who sat on it; the earth
and the heaven fled from his presence, and no place was
found for them" (Rv 20:11). The terrible presence of
God's glory on his throne is under the canopy of his
mercy, the rainbow. Angelic, priestly figures surround
the Lord, praising him, falling to the ground, and casting
the crowns of their glory before his throne.

God is king and judge, but merciful in
judgement, and he is also the bridegroom welcoming
his bride Israel, not transformed into the ecclesia.
"Every creature in heaven and on earth and under the
earth and in the sea, and all that is in them" sing to the
Father on the throne and to his Son the Lamb, "blessing
and honor and glory and might forever and ever" (Rv
5:13). This eternal and joyous song expresses God's
singing silence. It is the primal silence of the end, which
silence sings in the recreation. The living and the dead
are brought before the throne and "judged according to
their words, as recorded in the book of life" (Rv 20:12).
God judges each according to his or her character, that
is, their basic inclination to love God or to turn away
from him. The Lord takes the martyrs robed in white

and others who love him to dwell with him forever; he sends those who choose not to love him away eternally.

Most significantly, St. John tells the faithful what they can expect in Heaven. They would, he said, eat from the Tree of Life, and God Himself would, "wipe away every tear from their eyes, and death shall be no more, neither shall there be mourning nor crying nor pain any more, for the former things have passed away" (Rev 21:4).

Further insights into Heaven are provided in the Epistles. St. Luke's *Acts of the Apostles* begins with Jesus' Ascension into Heaven, reinforcing the Jewish teaching of an afterlife in Heaven—a Heaven where the Patriarch's are already resting. From St. Stephen's vision of Jesus sitting at the right hand of the Father in Heaven to St. Paul's constant exhortations for man to prepare for the coming of the Kingdom, Luke's text embraces the concept of Heaven as a reward for a life lived in Christian faith.

In the Epistle of St. James, we again find the promise of personal reward in Heaven: "Happy the man who holds out to the end through trial! Once he has been proven, he will receive the crown of life the Lord has promised to those who love Him" (James 1:12).

St. Peter speaks in his first Epistle of the "imperishable inheritance, incapable of fading or defilement, which is kept in heaven for you (1 Pet 1:3)," and maintains that "the God of all grace, who called you to his everlasting glory in Christ, will himself restore, confirm, strengthen, and establish those who have suffered a little while. Dominion be His throughout the ages" (1 Pet 5:11). Like St. John, St. Peter speaks in his second Epistle of a new Heaven and a new earth: "What we await are a new heavens and a new earth, where, according to his promise, the justice of God will reside" (2 Pet 3:13).

Essentially, the Epistles, like the Gospels, treat the fundamental Christian concept of Heaven as being a home for the redeemed. For those who arrive, the beatific vision of God is the ultimate reward. But the Epistles not only dwell on Heaven's grandeur and glory, but on its love as well. Only in Heaven will the conditions of love be fulfilled. For only then will the children of God be fully reunited with their Father. To better explain this Heaven God intended especially for us, St. Paul uses the following analogy: "We know that when the earthly tent in which we dwell is destroyed we have a dwelling provided for us by God, a dwelling in the heavens, not made by hands but to last forever. We groan while we are here, even as we yearn to have our heavenly habitation envelope us."

CHAPTER FIVE

THE COMMUNION OF SAINTS

The Old and New Testaments of Holy Scripture are the acknowledged repository of God's words to mankind. Therefore, the last word written in the New Testament signaled the completion of Divine Revelation. However, full understanding of God's Revelation wasn't immediate. Rather, it would slowly unfold over a long period of time. Not surprisingly, then, many of the Catholic books on Heaven draw not only from Holy Scripture and Sacred Church Tradition, but also from private revelation.

Not long after the death of St. John, the last living Apostle, a succession of devout, holy souls emerged to lead the Church into the future. Known as the Fathers of the Church, these early Christians were dynamic, spirit-filled leaders. Through their writings and actions, they helped shape and defend the early theological concepts of the Faith.

While such matters as the divinity of Christ and God's Trinitarian nature were at the heart of their work, the Fathers addressed the question of eternal life and what they believed the founders passed down to them about Heaven, Hell, and Purgatory.

From a Christian perspective, their teachings emphasized the primary theme of the Gospels and the Epistles concerning Heaven: Heaven's greatest joy was God Himself and man dwelling and being united with Him forever in love and peace. St. Cyprian referred to this true joy of heaven in saying, "How great will your glory and happiness be, to be allowed to see God, to be honored with sharing the joy of immorality in the Kingdom of Heaven with the righteous and God's friends."

However, according to scholars, the Church's teachings on

Heaven in the first several centuries underwent progressive development. Due to the vast persecution of Christians during this period, such a great loss of life needed to be understood in a way that helped the living accept and cope with the ever present prospect of martyrdom. Therefore, looking to the next life as one filled with reward for the losses in this one became more meaningful.

St. Irenaeus of Lyons, known for his *Adversus Haereses* treatise, is especially cited for such teachings. Considered the first great Catholic theologian, Irenaeus personally experienced the Roman persecutions at Lyons and taught that, indeed, Heaven would be so wonderful that it would clearly offset the disadvantages of this life, including unjust and premature death. As time passed and the General Resurrection so anticipated by early Christians failed to occur, not only a fuller understanding of martyrdom's reward but life after death was developed by the early Fathers.

Questions such as whether souls went directly to Heaven at death and whether they would enjoy eternal reward before the General Resurrection were questions that were now confronted . It was believed that the blessed were assured Heaven, but disagreements over the specifics emerged. St. Justin believed souls could not enjoy Heaven until the Resurrection, while St. Ignatius, like St. Irenaeus, felt that the martyrs' merits placed them in such favor with God that not only would they enter the abode of the blessed before the General Resurrection, but some would have higher places in Heaven than others. Jeffery Burton Russell writes of this era in Christian history:

> Justin set the Judeo-Christian resurrection of the body against the Greek immortality of the soul. He insisted on the resurrected body and its identity with the present body. This was in part a response to the gnostic denial of the body's value. Justin argued that the salvation proclaimed to humanity is proclaimed to human flesh. The body inherits the kingdom; even more, the kingdom inherits the flesh. Irenaeus (second century) reaffirmed this view strongly, but his near-contemporary Arthenagoras attempted to quell Greco-Roman philosophical objections by accommodating bodily resurrection to the immorality of the soul. On

the one hand, he accepted the resurrection of the body; on the other, he claimed that in heaven, even after the resurrection of the body, we shall live with God as heavenly spirits.

Iranaeus summed up the tradition as it was in his time. All the blessed in heaven will see Christ, the glory of the communion of saints, and the renovation of the world. They will dwell in their true home, where with Christ they enjoy eternal peace and comfort. Paradise, the heavenly city, the celestial abode, and the reign of God will come together at the end of time, when the Word of God restores the cosmos to himself. We were originally created in Eden in God's image and likeness, and the grace of the Holy Spirit will restore and further perfect that blessed state. The image (*imago*) is the natural image of God intrinsic in every human soul; the likeness (*similitudo*) is the potential, through grace, of becoming like him in eternal life.

Later writers would fall in line with Iranaeus. Origon (185-254), Lactantius (260-330), and St. Augustine (354-430) all wrote of such matters, as Christian literature firmly established Heaven as an abode of peace, an eternal home with God, filled with joy, beauty, light , peace, and happiness in Christ. The joy of meeting our loved ones as well as Heaven's heroes also became part of a Christian's interest in Heaven.

Over the first five centuries, the Christian concept of Heaven continued to develop. The Church confronted such questions as whether or not souls in Heaven would remember their earthly lives, their sins, and painful memories. They also wondered about the nature of the soul and its relationship to the body (at the Resurrection and in Heaven), the presence or absence of guilt, whether "just" pagans who lived before and after Christ went to Heaven, human sexuality in the resurrected body, the purgation of the soul, the difference between the Personal and General Judgements, the degree of heavenly gifts (such as knowledge and wisdom), heavenly relationships, who God in Heaven was and how souls would love Him there, the fate of the universe, the makeup of the glorified body, what our personalities and identities would be like in Heaven, and whether or not evil could totally be removed in a soul. The latter issue had to do, more or less, with the eternal fate of the damned and whether or not they could ever enter Heaven.

After the end of the Roman persecutions, the Christian idea of Heaven expanded even more. This time it was not because of danger and political oppression, but through and because of faith and liturgical practices. The Creed and the Mass offered more information on the nature of Paradise. The Church acknowledged the faithful's need for a concrete image of the promised afterlife in Christ. What life in Heaven was like, specifically, also continued to be confronted. More questions emerged, such as what age people were in Heaven, how they perceived God (without eyes and human senses), and how the body and soul separated at death. These were all topics of debate. As it still is today, the profound mystery of the beatific vision was being contemplated.

Similar to what occurred in the second and third centuries, visual concepts of Heaven were especially noted in the art work of this era. Mary's Assumption into Heaven, an idea already well established by the fourth century, was a common theme represented in many depictions of Heaven. In most, the blessed are seen in communal joy with their Queen. Artistic renditions of this mystery also revealed symbolic representations of Heaven, which showed the Trinity in relationship to Heaven's members. Halos, angels, clouds, and other images were captured in works of art, thereby placing in the minds of the faithful images of such heavenly considerations.

With the advent of monasteries, urban centers, and universities, the early Middle Ages spawned concepts of Heaven compatible with *Genesis* and the *Book of Revelation*. Both agrarian and urban lifestyles were compared to what Heaven would be like. For some, the restoration of Paradise as it was in the beginning was likened to Heaven. For others, Heaven was seen as a great urban center, fulfilling Revelation's prophecy of the great heavenly city, the New Jerusalem.. A planned city-state rich in gardens and orderly homes and streets provided a concrete image for many who wondered what Heaven must be like.

Visionaries and Church leaders added to the pool of ideas and thoughts about the nature of Heaven, as did poets and artists. Medieval literature promoted Heaven as a city-state with a court organized around God. The laity and the clergy moved about like travelers glimpsing the different realms or levels of Heaven. Socially, Heaven was seen as both horizontal and vertical, with the overwhelming theme of the reported visions emphasizing how the human eye and mind was unable to grasp the majesty and glory of Heaven. By the 12th century, reported visions of Heaven were commonplace. Moreover, according to author Jeffrey Burton Russell, a clear and distinct concept of Purgatory as a lower, intern state of Heaven was also emerging:

> Visions of heaven proliferated in the 12th century. In 1110, a nine-year old Italian boy in Campania named Alberic had a vision in which he visited hell, purgatory, and an earthly paradise. Then he mounted through the seven planetary spheres to heaven, about which he was forbidden to speak upon his return. Gottschalk, a German peasant, had a vision in 1188 of hell, paradise, and heaven. On his journey he encountered people that he knew who had died. In 1196, an English monk of Eynsham in Oxfordshire was guided by Saint Nicholas through hell and purgatory. Nicholas, like Dante's Virgil later, left the monk, who then proceeded in to paradise by himself. In paradise the monk sees souls mounting to heaven, where he is himself unable to go. As with Dante, the monk's vision lasted from Thursday to Easter Monday.
>
> In the *Vision of Gunthelm*, an English Cistercian of the 12th century, Gunthelm, is shown two paradises. One is a place of great beauty; in its midst is a chapel, in which Mary sits on a throne with the elect surrounding her. Wearing a golden robe, she shines among them as the sun shines among the stars. Gunthelm then visits a second paradise with a beautiful door and golden walls set with jewels. Inside the walls of the city is the garden containing many kinds of plants and trees; birds sing amidst fragrant flowers and plenteous fruits. The imaging of paradise as a city when seen from outside and as garden when seen from inside appeared in poetry, art, liturgy, and public festival. Townspeople in the 12th century sometimes decorated their city on the feast of its

patron saint with fronds, greenery, and incense to represent the sweet smelling heavenly garden within the walled heavenly city.

Saint Patrick's Purgatory is the story of a knight named Owen who about 1150 descended into a cave that by tradition had been shown to Saint Patrick centuries before as the entrance of the other world. The story, written in Latin about 1180, enjoyed considerable popularity and was translated several times into the vernacular, once by the famous poet Marie de France. Owen's experience, like Brendan's is presented not as a vision but as an actual physical journey. Without a guide be passes by the gate of hell then crosses a bridge and enters through a jeweled gate in to the earthly paradise, where the light is brighter than the sun. He meets a procession of clergy bound for heaven, bearing crosses, banners, candles, and golden palm fronds, and singing in a mode unknown on earth. In monastic literature, monks, Saint Peter, or angels led the voyager, but here two archbishops lead Owen through lush and flowered meadows on which trees were bearing fruit whose scent nourished him. It is a land where no discomfort of any kind can exist. The archbishops take Owen to a mountain from whose peak he sees a golden sky. A flame "descended on the head of the knight and entered him just as it entered the others. Then he felt such a sweet sense of delight in his body and his heart that he could scarcely tell, for the delight of the sweetness, whether he was living or dead; but time passed in an instant." Owen wants to stay, but the archbishops send him back to this world, promising him that if he converts and leads a good life he will return to heaven at his death.

The trend toward the institutional imagery of the visible church on earth is clear in the figures of the two guiding archbishops and the preference shown the clergy in general. The earthly paradise has become a prequel to the celestial one. With the growth of the idea of purgatory, this meant two varieties of interstate, one for the already blessed souls awaiting the resurrection in peace; the other for those who need a greater cleansing before they can enjoy beatitude. Implied is the idea that souls are released from purgatory once they are sufficiently purified and then repair to the earthly paradise, there to await the resurrection happily. A narrative sequence has developed; death; separation of soul from body; particular judgment; purgatory or else earthly paradise; resurrection; reunion of body and soul; final judgement; final bliss in heaven. The sequence describes, in both overt and symbolic senses, the process of "going to heaven."

By the thirteenth century, theologians were also sharpening the view of Heaven. St. Thomas Aquinas's writings crystallized what souls could expect when they arrived there. Aquinas presented a systematic presentation of Heaven in a complete form which viewed Heaven as an experience, most of all, of the intellect. Aquinas visioned the glorified human body to be like the glorified Christ in Scripture, but warned that not all the blessed would be equally luminous or of the same clarity. There were no plants or animals in Heaven and movement would cease, he wrote.

Emphasizing much of Augustine's teachings on Heaven, Aquinas tried to present a true doctrine. He believed there would be no active life in Heaven and that contemplation would be perfect. Knowledge of God would thus be supreme and this, in essence, would be perfect bliss. Knowing God would be the final act of a human, and with such perfect knowledge, would then come perfect happiness. Again, each soul in Heaven would possess a different degree of such knowledge but the completeness of their beatitude would still be perfect for them. They would have no reality of their deficiency, asserted Aquinas. In addition, Aquinas believed there would be two other sources of happiness besides God: the restored body and the community of the blessed. These would make the afterlife, more or less, perfect.

Other theologians of the 13th century disagreed with Aquinas. Giles of Rome (1247-1316), Aquinas's student, felt that there would be a perfect "society" in Heaven and that this would be part of the bliss. While St. Bonaventure (1221-1274) thought there would be "special friends" in Heaven, something Aquinas could not foresee.

During this period there also emerged more profound concepts of the love to be experienced in Heaven. The images of courtly love, best known in the revelations of St. Gertrude, in which the Lord was viewed as a spouse, appeared in many writings and visions. This imaging gave way to an experience of Heaven that transcended human passion but sought to establish the concept of a soul being united like a bride to Christ. Once a soul was united, it then supposedly experienced the sweetness and beauty of God Himself in a higher form of divine love. This love implied submission, service, loyalty, and obedience to Christ. Thus, Heaven, as a whole, was a social state, a society of love. While these concepts today are still a part of many visions of Heaven, they were never considered as true theological teaching. McDannell and Lang address this issue in *Heaven, A History*:

> While the visions of medieval mystics such as Mechtild and Gertrude are provocative and enchanting, they never became a part of the canon of Christian teaching. Their visions, unlike the theology of Thomas Aquinas, remained basically a private form of spirituality. Later writers within the mystical tradition, however, would use similar themes to discuss the intimate relationship between God and the soul in heaven. The clarity and abstract nature of Aquinas's thought on celestial matters would become standard in Catholic theology, but the emotion-filled   richness of afterlife visions would invigorate each generation of heavenly speculations. Although at times there would be tension between the intellectual, abstract heaven of the theologians and the emotional, colorful heaven of the mystics, for the most part these two perspectives would coexist peacefully. The theological heaven would be voiced in the public space of the university, seminary, and pulpit, and the mystical heaven in the private space of the diary, cloister, confessional, and chapel.

By the 17th century, the concept of a theocratic Heaven was well established in western Christianity. However, the sensuality of the Renaissance was now being replaced by a God-dominated Heaven in which, once again, eternal life was viewed primarily as an intimate relationship with the divine.

The Catechism of the Council of Trent, which was published by the decree of Pope St. Pius V in 1566, recognized and asserted the Christian teaching of the reward of everlasting life and what this hope embraced. The articles of the Catechism defined the resurrection of the body, its glorious restoration, and the qualities of its immorality. Moreover, it confirmed that the blessedness and joy of possessing everlasting life was essentially in seeing God. The Council summarized the enjoyment of His beauty, goodness, and perfection:

> Solid happiness, which we may designate by the common appellation, *essential*, consists in the vision of God, and the enjoyment of His beauty who is the source and principle of all goodness and perfection. *This*, says Christ our Lord, *is eternal life: that they may know thee, the only true God, and Jesus Christ, whom thou hast sent.* These words St. John seems to interpret when he says: *Dearly beloved, we are now the sons of God; and it hath not yet appeared what we shall be. We know that when he shall appear, we shall be like to him: because we shall see him as he is.* He shows, then, beatitude consists of two things: that we shall behold God as He is in His own nature and substance; and that we ourselves shall become as it were, gods.

The Light of Glory

Those who enjoy God while retaining their own nature assume a certain admirable and almost divine form, the forms of gods rather than of men. Why this transformation takes place becomes at once intelligible if we only consider that a thing is known either from its essence or from its image and appearance. Consequently, as nothing so resembles God as to afford by its resemblance a perfect knowledge of Him, it follows that no creature can behold His Divine Nature and Essence unless this same Divine Essence has joined itself to us, and this St. Paul means when he says: "We now see through a glass in the dark manner, but then face to face." St. Augustine understands the words, *in a dark manner,* to mean that we see Him in a resemblance calculated to convey to us some notion of the Deity.

This St. Denis also clearly shows when he says that the things above cannot be known by comparison with the things below; for the essence and substance of anything incorporeal cannot be known through the image of that which is corporeal, particularly as a resemblance must be less gross and more spiritual than that which it represents, as we easily know from universal experience. Since, therefore, it is impossible that any image drawn from created things should be equally pure and spiritual with God, no resemblance can enable us perfectly to comprehend the Divine Essence. Moreover, all created things are circumscribed within certain limits of perfection, while God is without limits, and therefore nothing created can reflect His immensity.

The only means, then, for arriving at a knowledge of the Divine Essence is that God unites Himself in some manner to us, and after, in some incomprehensible way, elevates our minds to a higher degree of perfection, and thus renders us capable of contemplating the beauty of His Nature. This will be accomplished by the light of His glory. Illuminated by its splendor we shall see God, the true light, in His own light.

The Beatific Vision

The blessed always see God and by this greatest and most exalted of gifts, being made *partakers of the divine nature,* they enjoy true and solid happiness. Our belief in this happiness should be joined with an assured hope that we too shall one day, through the divine goodness, attain it. This the Fathers declared in their

Creed, which says: *I expect the resurrection of the dead and the life of the world to come.*

An Illustration of This Truth

These are truths, so divine that they cannot be expressed in any words or comprehended by us in any thought. We may, however, trace some resemblance of this happiness in sensible objects. Thus, iron when acted on by fire becomes inflamed and while it is substantially the same, seems changed into fire, a different substance; so likewise the blessed, who are admitted into the glory of heaven and burn with a love of God, are so affected that, without ceasing to be what they are, they may be said with truth to differ more from those still on earth than red-hot iron differs from itself when cold.

Supreme and absolute happiness, which we can call essential, consists in the possession of God; for what can he lack to consummate his happiness who possesses the God of all goodness and perfection?

Accessory Happiness

To this happiness, however, are added certain gifts which are common to all the blessed, and which, because more within the reach of human comprehension, are generally found more effectual in moving and inflaming the heart. These the Apostle seems to have in view when, in his Epistle to the Romans, he says: *Glory and honour, and peace to every one that worketh good.*

Glory

For the blessed shall enjoy glory; not only that glory which we have already shown to continue essential happiness, or to be its inseparable accompaniment, but also that glory which consists in the clear and distinct knowledge which each (of the blessed) shall have of the singular and exalted dignity of his companions (in glory).

Honor

And how distinguished must not that honor be which is conferred by God Himself, who no longer calls them servants, but friends, brethren and sons of God! Hence the Redeemer will address His elect in these most loving and honorable words: *Come, ye blessed of my Father, possess you the kingdom prepared for you.* Justly, then, may we exclaim: *Thy friends, O God, are made exceedingly honourable.* They shall also receive the highest praise from Christ the Lord, in presence of His heavenly Father and His Angels.

And if nature has implanted in the heart of every man the common desire of securing the esteem of men eminent for wisdom, because they are deemed the most reliable judges of merit, what an accession of glory to the blessed, to show towards each other the highest veneration!

Peace

To enumerate all the delights with which the souls of the blessed shall be filled would be an endless task. We cannot even conceive them in thought. With this truth, however, the minds of the faithful should be deeply impressed —that the happiness of the Saints is full to overflowing of all those pleasures which can be enjoyed or even desired in this life, whether they regard the powers of them and/or of the perfection of the body; albeit this must be in a manner more exalted than, to use the Apostle's words, eye hath seen, ear heard, or the heart of man conceived.

Thus the body, which was before gross and material, shall put off in heaven its morality and having become refined and spiritualized, will no longer require corporal food; while the soul shall be satiated to its supreme delight with that eternal food of glory which the Master of that great feast passing will minister to all.

Who will desire rich apparel of royal robes, where there shall be no further use for such things, and where all shall be clothed with immorality and splendors, and adorned with a crown of imperishable glory.

And if the possession of a spacious and magnificent mansion contributes to human happiness, what more spacious, what more magnificent, can be conceived than heaven itself, which is illumined throughout with the brightness of God? Hence the Prophet, contemplating the beauty of his dwelling-place, and burning with the desire of reaching those mansions of bliss, exclaims: *How lovely are thy tabernacles, O Lord of hosts! My soul longeth and fainteth for the courts of the Lord. My heart and my flesh have rejoiced in the living God.*

That the faithful may be all filled with the same sentiments and utter the same language should be the object of the pastor's most earnest desires, as it should also of his zealous labors. For *in my Father's house,* says our Lord, *there are many mansions,* in which shall be distributed rewards of greater and of less value according to each one's deserts. *He who soweth sparingly, shall also reap sparingly, and he who soweth in blessings, shall also reap blessings.*

How to Arrive at Enjoyment of This Happiness

The pastor, therefore, should not only encourage the faithful to seek this happiness, but should frequently remind them that the sure way of obtaining it is to possess the virtues of faith and charity, to preserve in prayer and the use of Sacraments, and to discharge all the duties of kindness towards their neighbor.

Thus, through the mercy of God, who has prepared that blessed glory for those who love Him, shall be one day fulfilled the words of the Prophet: *My people shall sit in the beauty of peace, and in the tabernacle of confidence, and in wealthy rest.*

Since the Council of Trent, historians, theologians, poets,

artists, and visionaries have continued to present concepts of Heaven.
Science as a basis for proving Heaven, through numerous documented
after-death experiences, and the 20th century emphasis on the reuniting
of family in Heaven, have added new perspectives to the picture. But
for the most part, Heaven has not changed much in Catholic theology,
as is evidenced in the 1994 Catechism of the Catholic Church:

Heaven and Earth

The Apostles' Creed professes that God is
"Creator of heaven and earth." The Nicene Creed
makes it explicit that this profession includes "all that is,
seen and unseen."

The Scriptural expression "heaven and earth"
means all that exists, creation in its entirety. It also
indicates the bond, deep within creation, that both
unites heaven and earth and distinguishes the one from
the other: "the earth" is the world of men while
"heaven" or "the heavens" can designate both the
firmament and God's own "place," and consequently,
the "heaven" which is eschatological glory. Finally,
"heaven" refers to the saints and the "place" of the
spiritual creatures, the angels, who surround God.

The profession of faith of the Fourth Lateran
Council (1215) affirms that God "from the beginning of
time made at once (simul) out of nothing both orders of
creatures, the spiritual and the corporeal, that is, the
angelic and the earthly, and then (deinde) the human
creature, who as it were shares in both orders, being
composed of spirit and body."

Those who die in God's grace and friendship
and are perfectly purified live for ever with Christ. They
are like God forever, for they "see him as he is," face to
face:

> By virtue of our apostolic authority, we
> define the following: According to the
> general disposition of God, the souls of
> all the saints ... and other faithful who

died after receiving Christ's holy Baptism (provided they were not in need of purification when they died, ... or, if they then did need or will need some purification, when they have been purified after death....). Already before they take up their bodies again and before the general judgement —and this since the Ascension of our Lord and Savior Jesus Christ into heaven—have been, are, and will be in heaven, in the heavenly Kingdom and celestial paradise with Christ, joined to the company of the holy angels. Since the Passion and death of our Lord Jesus Christ, these souls have been sent and do see the divine essence with an intuitive vision, and even face to face, without the mediation of any creature.

This perfect life with the Most Holy Trinity— this communion of life and love with the Trinity, with the Virgin Mary, the angels and all the blessed—is called "heaven." Heaven is the ultimate end and fulfillment of the deepest human longings, the state of supreme, definitive happiness.

To live in heaven is "to be with Christ." The elect live "in Christ," but they retain, or rather find, their true identity, their own name.

By his death and Resurrection, Jesus Christ has "opened" heaven to us. The life of the blessed consists in the full and perfect possession of the fruits of the redemption accomplished by Christ. He makes partners in his heavenly glorification those who have believed in him and remained faithful to his will. Heaven is the blessed community of all who are perfectly incorporated into Christ.

This mystery of blessed communion with God

and all who are in Christ is beyond all understanding and description. Scripture speaks of it in images: life, light, peace, wedding feast, wine of the kingdom, the Father's house, the heavenly Jerusalem, and paradise: "no eye has seen, nor ear heard, nor the heart of man conceived, what God has prepared for those who love him."

Because of his transcendence, God cannot be seen as he is, unless he himself opens up this mystery of man's immediate contemplation and gives him the capacity for it. The Church calls this contemplation of God in his heavenly glory "the beatific vision":

How great will your glory and happiness be, to be allowed to see God, to be honored with sharing the joy of salvation and eternal light with Christ your Lord and God...to delight in the joy of immortality in the Kingdom of Heaven with the righteous and God's friends.

In the glory of heaven the blessed continue joyfully to fulfill God's will in relation to other men and to all creation. Already they reign with Christ; with him "they shall reign for ever and ever.

Thus, since the earliest days of the Church, Heaven for each generation of Christians has essentially remained the same. Heaven is God above us, with us, and within us. It is joy, a place of indescribable beauty, and it is governed by love. Love, essentially, rules Heaven. Indeed, the Christian can expect to be forever happy in the contemplation of God alone, who is the source of all love.

CHAPTER SIX

VISIONS OF HEAVEN

As early as the 2nd century, there are documented reports of Christians receiving dreams and visions of Heaven. These early revelations were captivating and, as they remain to this day, controversial. This is because Church authorities have historically frowned on what the faithful embrace outside of Divine Revelation. But such reports today are undeniably popular, and it was no different in the early Church.

The most noted accounts of celestial visions from the first several centuries are *The Shepherd of Hermas,* a vision describing the opening of Heaven, where martyrs and angels are seen living joyfully with Christ; *The Vision of Paul*, a story of an angelic guided tour of the celestial Paradise; and the classic *Passion of Perpetua*, visions of Paradise through the eyes of expectant martyrs which reveal Heaven to be a world of peace, light, and happiness.

Christ and his angels are at the center of Perpetua's accounts. The symbolism the visions convey was intended to increase the excitement and anticipation of expectant martyrs at a difficult time in Christian history. The record of the passion of St. Perpetua, St. Felicity, and her companions, which includes several reported visions of the afterlife, was so highly esteemed in the ancient Church that St. Augustine protested, arguing that the visions were being equated with Holy Scripture. Butler's *Lives of the Saints* gives the following account of the heavenly visions of St. Saturus, one of St. Perpetua's companion:

St. Saturus also had a vision which he described in writing. He and his companions were conducted by angels into a beautiful garden, where they met martyrs named Jocundus, Saturninus and Artaxius, who had lately been burnt alive and Quintus, who had died in prison. Then they were led to a place which seemed as though it were built of light, and sitting in it was One white-haired with the face of a youth—"whose feet we saw not"—and on His right and on His left and behind Him were many elders, and all sang with one voice, "Holy, holy, holy." They stood before the throne, and "we kissed Him, and he passed His hand over our faces. And the other elders said to us, 'Stand up.' And we stood up and gave the kiss of peace. And the elders said to us, 'Go and play.'" Then Saturus said of Perpetua, "You have all you desired"; and she replied, "Thanks be to God that as I was merry in the flesh, so am I still merrier here." He adds that as they went out they found before the gate their bishop, Optatus, and Aspasius, a priest, alone and sorrowful. They fell at the martyrs' feet and begged them to reconcile them, for they had quarreled. As Perpetua was talking to them in Greek, "beneath a rose-tree," the angels told the two clerics to compose their differences, and charged Optatus to heal the factions in his church. Saturus adds: "We began to recognize many brethren and martyrs there, and we all drew strength from an inexpressible fragrance which delighted us; and in joy I awoke."

While the *Acts of St. Perpetua* are ancient, they read much the same as the visions of Heaven recorded in the lives of the saints and faithful over the centuries. From the 3rd century accounts of St. Catherine of Alexandria (the same St. Catherine who came to St. Joan of Arc) being carried off bodily to Heaven by angels to the sixth century writings of St. Gregory the Great, whose visions of Heaven are recorded in his classic, *Dialogues*, the early Church was filled with short, yet vivid stories of individuals who reportedly had heavenly experiences.

Published towards the end of 593 AD, St. Gregory's *Dialogues* became one of the most popular books of the Middle Ages. The book combined stories of visions, prophecies, and miracles that were collected from oral tradition and spontaneously assembled to form evidence in favor of the supernatural. Over the centuries, St. Gregory has been criticized for this work, but defenders claim that he lived in a very credulous time. One account was of a soldier in Rome who claimed to have visited Heaven:

> Across the bridge there were green and pleasant meadows carpeted with sweet flowers and herbs. In the fields, groups of white-clothed people were seen. Such a sweet scent filled the air that it fed those who dwelt and walked there. The dwellings of the blessed were full of a great light. A house of amazing capacity was being constructed there, apparently out of golden bricks, but he could not find out for whom it might be.

As noted, the private revelations of the Popes, mystics, and saints during this period are highly criticized today for not being more closely discerned. To many such stories, critics say, were recorded indiscriminately. But such accounts of visions and dreams of Heaven, as rendered by some of the more popular and recognizable saints, are an established part of the glorious Catholic tradition about Heaven.

Over the centuries, Church history records that many of its saints received visions of Heaven. St. Anthony the Abbot (251-356), known as St. Anthony of the Desert, reported seeing a vision of St. Paul the Hermit's (d.342) soul ascending into Heaven among an assembly of angels and holy souls. St. Christina the Astonishing (1150-1224) of Brusthem, Belgium, relayed an ecstatic experience in a church that caused her, while levitating in mid air, to visit Heaven and experience its peace, love, and glory. Christina even claimed to view the throne of God.

St. Margaret of Cortona, a 13th century resident of Tuscany, said that on her deathbed she saw, coming to escort her, a great number of souls from Paradise who were there because of her intercessions. St. Gertrude the Great, another 13th century saint, also described a vision of an angelic escort coming from Heaven for her. Likewise, comes the story of St. Clara of Montefelco who reported a heavenly vision that revealed the Most Holy Trinity. St. Lydwina of Schiedam, Holland, (1380-1433) did not claim to see God but to have visited with the saints in Heaven, as did a man named Blasio Massei, who was raised from the dead by St. Bernadine of Siena (1380-1444). Blasio, too, saw the throne of God surrounded by angels and towered over by the Blessed Virgin Mary. Even the great 14th century saint, St. Catherine of Siena, experienced visions of Heaven: "I have seen the hidden things of God and now I am thrust back into the prison of the body."

The following revelations of Heaven were recorded over the past millennium. These accounts were chosen not so much for their visual imagery of Heaven, which is found in almost all such accounts, but for their spiritual profoundness. Each offers a different insight or perspective of the Kingdom to come.

St. Dominic

Dominic Guzman, better known as St. Dominic, was born in 1170 and died in 1221. St. Dominic was a friend of St. Francis of Assisi and, like St. Francis, lived a life of miracles. He reported the following vision of God in Heaven:

> Now the blessed Dominic returned to pray in the place where he was before, and scarcely had he begun to pray when he was wrapt in spirit unto God. And he saw the Lord, with the Blessed Virgin standing on His right hand; and it seemed to him that Our Lady was dressed in a robe of sapphire blue. And looking about him, he saw religious of every order standing before God; but of his own he did not see one. Then he began to weep bitterly, and he dared not draw nigh to Our Lord or to His Mother; but Our Lady beckoned him with her hand to approach. Nevertheless, he did not dare to come until Our Lord also in His turn had made him a sign to do so. He came, therefore, and fell prostrate before them, weeping bitterly. And the Lord commanded him to rise; and when he was risen, He said to him, "Why weepest thou thus bitterly?" And he answered, "I weep because I see here religious of all orders except mine own." And the Lord said to him, "Wouldst thou see thine own?" And he, trembling, replied "Yes, Lord." Then the Lord placed His hand on the shoulder of the Blessed Virgin, and said to the blessed Dominic, "I have given thine Order to My Mother." Then He said again, "And wouldst thou really see thine order?" And he replied, "Yea, Lord." Then the Blessed Virgin opened the mantle

in which she seemed to be dressed, and extending it before the eyes of Dominic, so that its immensity covered all the space of the heavenly country, he saw under its folds a vast multitude of his friars.

The blessed Dominic fell down to thank God and the Blessed Mary, His Mother, and the vision disappeared, and he came to himself again and rang the bell for matins; and when matins were ended, he called them all together and made them a beautiful discourse on the love and veneration they should bear to the most Blessed Virgin, and related to them this vision.

St. Birgetta of Sweden

St. Birgetta of Sweden (also called St. Brigid) was a major figure in the Church of the late Middle Ages. Born in 1302 or 1303, she experienced her first vision at age seven. In her, *Book of Questions*, a book of heavenly revelations, she described the following vision of Heaven:

I saw a throne in the sky, and on it sat the Lord Jesus Christ as Judge. Before his feet sat the Virgin Mary; and around the throne, there was an army of angels and an infinite multitude of saints. A religious, very learned in theology, stood on a high rung of a ladder which was fixed in the earth and whose summit touched the sky. His gestures were very impatient and restless, as if he were full of guile and malice. He questioned the Judge, saying:

First question. "O Judge, I ask you: You have given me a mouth. May I not say the things that please me?"

Second question. "You have given me eyes. May I not see with them those things that delight me?"

Third question. "You have given me ears. Why am I not to hear with them those things that please me?"

Fourth question. "You have given me hands. Why am I not to do with them what agrees with me?"

Fifth question. "You have given me feet. Why shall I not walk with them as I desire?"

Christ's response to the first question. The Judge, who sat on the throne and whose gestures were meek and very dignified, replied: "Friend, I gave you a mouth that you might speak rationally about things that are useful for your body and soul and about things that belong to my honor."

Response to the second question. "Second, I gave you eyes that you might see evils to be fled and healthful things to be kept."

Response to the third question. "Third, I gave you ears that you might hear those things that belong to truth and honesty."

Response to the fourth question. "Fourth, I gave you hands that with them you might do those things that are necessary for the body and not harmful to the soul."

Response to the fifth question. "Fifth, I gave you feet that you might draw back from love of the world and go to your soul's rest with love of me, your Creator and Redeemer."

St. Rita of Cascia

About seventy-five miles from Rome, in the southeastern part of Umbria, sits the ancient city of Cascia. There, on May 22, 1381, was born St. Rita. Known as the Saint of the Impossible, St. Rita was a 14th century mystic and stigmatist who reported a vision of Heaven.

On the night of the day of her espousals with her divine Fiancé, through the three vows of religion, St. Rita was the recipient of a singular favor that made her supremely happy and pointed out to her a sure way to arrive at the port of the eternal salvation. As she was kneeling before the crucifix in her little cell, she saw in a vision, as the

Patriarch Jacob saw in a sleep, a ladder standing upon the
earth, and the top thereof touching Heaven. Gazing
attentively at the ladder, she observed God at the top of the
ladder inviting her to ascend, and she also saw angels
ascending and descending by it. While contemplating the
spectacle, she heard a voice which said to her: "Rita, if you
wish to unite yourself to God in Heaven, you must climb
this ladder." When the vision disappeared, St. Rita felt
much consoled and was filled with heavenly transports
because she had seen God, though it was only for a brief
moment.

St. Rita began, at once, to consider the mystery of
the ladder she had seen in the vision, and remembering that
they were angels who ascended and descended by it, she
came to understand that she must become like them if she
would follow in their footsteps. Penetrating deeper into the
mystery, the very steps of the ladder taught that she herself
must build at once a spiritual ladder, on whose steps, made
of virtues, she could ascend to Heaven, and enjoy there, for
all eternity, the presence and the companionship of God.

Juliana of Norwick

Juliana of Norwick was another 14th century mystic whose
recorded dialogue with God is still considered a mystical classic. In one of
her revelations, she explained how Heaven was shown to her so she might
better understand the reason Christ suffered for souls—a suffering that was
necessary for souls to attain the eternal Kingdom:

Then our good Lord Jesus Christ asked me, "Are
you really pleased that I suffered for you?"

I said, "Yes, good Lord, thank you so much! Yes,
good Lord, blessed may you be!"

Then our good, kind Lord Jesus said, "If you are
satisfied, I am satisfied. It is a joy, a bliss, an endless delight
to me that I ever suffered the passion for you, and if I could
suffer more, I would."

In feeling this, my understanding was lifted up into
heaven and there I saw three heavens. I was greatly

astounded at this sight, and thought I saw three heavens, all in the blessed manhood of Christ, none of them was greater, none was less, none was higher, none was lower, but all were equally alike in bliss.

For the first heaven, Christ showed me his Father—in no bodily likeness—but in his properties and in his working. That is to say, I saw in Christ what the Father is. The working of the Father is that he gives reward to his Son, Jesus Christ. This gift and this reward is so blissful to Jesus that his Father could have given him no reward that could have pleased him better. The first heaven, which is the pleasing of the Father, was shown to me as a heaven. It was completely blissful because he is completely pleased with all the deeds Jesus has done for our salvation.

Therefore, we are his not only because he has bought us but also by the courteous gift of his Father. We are his bliss, we are his reward; we are his glory, we are his crown. It was a singular marvel and a thing most delightful to behold, that we are his crown. All of this (which I have just said) is so great a joy to Jesus that for it he counts all his painful labor, his difficult passion, his cruel and shameful death, as nothing.

In the words, "If I could suffer more, I would," I saw in truth that he would have died as often as he could have, and love would never have let him rest until he had done it. I looked with great diligence to learn how often he would die if he could, and in truth, the number exceeded the power of my understanding and my wits to such an extent that my reason might not and could not comprehend it or take it in.

And even when he had died, or would have died, this many times, he still would count it as nothing for love, for all seems to him very small compared to his love.

Though the sweet manhood of Christ could suffer only once, the goodness in him can never cease offering itself: he is ready to do the same thing every day, if such a thing were possible. If he said he would, for my love, make new heavens and a new earth, it would be a very small thing compared to this, for he could do that every day if he wanted to, without any painful labor, but to die so often for my love that the number goes beyond created reason is the greatest offer our Lord God could make to man's soul, as I see it.

By all this he meant the following to be understood: "How should it, then, be that, for your love, I should not do all I could? The deed does not distress me, since for your love I should die so often with no regard for my intense pain."

For the second heaven, I saw here, looking at the blessed passion, that the love that made him suffer exceeds all his pains by as much as heaven is above earth. For the pain was a noble glorious deed done at a single time by the working of love, and love was without a beginning is, and shall be without an ending. For this love he said most sweetly these words: "If I could suffer more, I would." He did say, "If it were necessary to suffer more," because even though it were not necessary, if he could suffer more, he would. This deed and this work concerning our salvation was ordained as well as God could ordain it. And here I saw complete bliss in Christ, for his bliss would not have been complete if it could have been done better.

Mary of Agreda

The Venerable Mary of Agreda lived in the 17th century (1602-1663) and is best known for her classic, *The Mystical City of God*. In ecstasy, she wrote of the events of the Blessed Virgin Mary's life and many sublime mysteries of the faith, including Lucifer's rebellion, the hidden life of the Holy Family, the location of Hell and, of course, Heaven. Although her observations in this account are not of Heaven per se, it is very revealing of the abode of the blessed:

The Queen of all creatures was called from her resting place by a loud voice of the Most High, which strongly and sweetly raised Her above all created things and caused Her to feel new effects of divine power; for this was one of the most singular and admirable ecstasies of her most holy life. Immediately also She was filled with new enlightenment and divine influences, such as I have described in other places, until She reached the clear vision of the Divinity. The veil fell and She saw intuitively the Godhead itself in such glory and plenitude of insight, as all the capacity of men and angels could not describe or fully understand. All the knowledge of the Divinity and humanity of her most holy Son, which She had ever received in former visions was renewed and moreover, other secrets of the inexhaustible archives of the bosom of God were revealed to Her. I have not ideas or words sufficient and adequate for expressing what I have been allowed to see of these sacraments by the divine light; and their abundance and multiplicity convince me of the poverty and want of proper expression in created language.

The Most High announced to his Virgin Mother, that the time of his coming into the world had arrived and what would be the manner in which this was now to be fulfilled and executed. The most prudent Lady perceived in this vision the purpose and exalted scope of these wonderful mysteries and sacraments, as well in so far as related to the Lord himself as also in so far as they concerned creatures, for whose benefit they had even primarily decreed. She prostrated Herself before the throne of his Divinity and gave Him glory, magnificence, thanks, and praise for Herself and for all creatures, such as was befitting the ineffable mercy and condescension of his divine love. At the same time She asked of the divine majesty new light and grace in order to be able worthily to undertake the service and worship and the rearing up of the Word made flesh, whom She was to bear in Her arms and nourish with her virginal milk.. This petition the heavenly Mother brought forward with the profoundest humility of Mother of God. He commanded Her to exercise this office and ministry of a legitimate and true Mother of Himself; that She should treat Him as the Son of the Eternal Father and at the same time the Son of her womb. All this could be easily entrusted to such a Mother, in whom was contained an excellence that words cannot express.

The most holy Mary remained in this ecstasy and beatific vision for over an hour immediately preceding her divine delivery.

Venerable Anne Catherine Emmerich

Anne Catherine Emmerich was born near Koesfeld, Westphalia, in West Germany on September 8, 1774. She became a nun of the Augustinian Order and is known today as perhaps the greatest mystic of her times. She bore the stigmata, lived only on the holy Eucharist for twelve years, and recorded some of the most profound visions in the history of the Church. Excerpts of these visions are provided in the following passages:

> I saw spreading out before me a boundless, resplendent space, above which floated a globe of light shining like a sun. I felt that It was the Unity of the Trinity. In my own mind, I named It the one voice, and I watched It producing Its effects. Below the globe of light arose concentric circles of radiant choirs of spirits, wondrously bright and strong and beautiful. This second world of light floated like a sun under that higher Sun.
>
> These choirs came forth from the higher Sun, as if born of love. Suddenly I saw some of them pause, rapt in the contemplation of their own beauty. They took complacency in self, they sought the highest beauty in self, they thought but of self, they existed but in self.
>
> At first all were lost in contemplation out of self, but soon some of them rested in self. At this instant, I saw this part of the glittering choirs hurled down, their beauty sunk in darkness, while the others, thronging quickly together, filled up their vacant places. And now the good angels occupied a smaller space. I did not see them leaving their places to pursue and combat the fallen choirs. The bad angels rested in self and fell away, while those that did not follow their example thronged into their vacant places. All this was instantaneous.
>
> Then rising from below, I saw a dark disc, the future abode of the fallen spirits. I saw that they took possession of it against their will. It was much smaller than

the sphere from which they had fallen, and they appeared
to me to be closely crowded together.

I saw the Fall of the angels in my childhood and
ever after, day and night, I dreaded their influence. I
thought they must do great harm to the earth, for they are
always around it. It is well they have not bodies, else they
would obscure the light of the sun. We should see them
floating around us like shadows.

Immediately after the Fall, I saw the spirits in the
shining circles humbling themselves before God. They did
homage to Him and implored pardon for the fallen angels.

At that moment I saw a movement in the
luminous sphere in which God dwelt. Until then it had
been motionless and, as I felt, awaiting that prayer. After
that action on the part of the angelic choirs, I felt assured that
they would remain steadfast, that they would never fall
away. It was made known to me that God in His
judgment, in His eternal sentence against the rebel angels,
decreed the reign of strife until their vacant thrones are
filled. But to fill those thrones seemed to me almost
impossible, for it would take so long. The strife will
however be upon the earth. There will be no strife above,
for God has so ordained.

After I had received this assurance, I could no
longer sympathize with Lucifer, for I saw that he had cast
himself down by his own free, wicked will. Neither could
I feel such anger against Adam or the contrary. I felt
sympathy for him because I thought: It has been thus
ordained.

As we mounted I beheld the Archangel Michael
floating above me. The sky became clearer and of a more
beautiful blue, and I saw the sun and the other heavenly
bodies as I had seen them before in a vision. We went
around the whole earth and through all the celestial worlds,
in which I saw innumerable gardens with their fruits and
signification. I hope some time to be allowed to enter, for
I want to get medicines and recipes to cure pious sick
people. I saw the choirs of the blessed and sometimes, here

and there, a saint standing in his sphere with his own distinctive insignia. Still souring upward, we arrived at a world of unspeakably wonderful magnificence. It was shaped like a dome, like an azure disc, surrounded by a ring of light above which were nine other rings on every one of which rested a throne. These circles were full of angels. From the thrones arose many-colored arches filled with fruits, precious stones, and costly gifts of God, which met in a dome surmounted by three angelic thrones. The middle one was St. Michael's. Thither he flew and placed the tabernacle on top of the dome. Each of the three angels, Michael, Gabriel, and Raphael stood over a part of the dome formed by three of the nine angelic choirs, and four great, luminous angels, veiled with their wings, moved constantly around them. They are the Elohim: Raphial, Etophiel, Emmanuel, and Salathiel, the administrators and distributors of God's superabundant graces, which they receive from the three archangels and scatter throughout the Church, to the four points of the compass. Gabriel and Raphael were in long, white robes like a priest's. Michael wore a helmet with a crest of rays, and his body seemed encased in armor and girt with cords, his robe descending to the knees like a fringed apron. In one hand he held a long staff surmounted by a cross under which floated the standard of the Lamb; in the other was a flaming sword. His feet also were laced.

Above the dome lay a still higher world in which I saw the Most Blessed Trinity represented by three figures: the Father, an old man like a high-priest, presenting to His Son on His right the orb of the world; the Son who held a cross in one hand; and to the left of the Father stood a luminous winged figure. Around them sat twenty-four ancients in a circle. The cherubim and seraphim with many other spirits stood around the throne of God hymning incessant praise.

In the center above Michael, stood Mary surrounded by innumerable circles of luminous souls, angels, and virgins. The grace of Jesus flows through Mary to the three archangels, each of whom radiates three kinds of gifts upon three of the nine inferior choirs. These in their turn, pour them forth upon all nature and the whole human race.

As the tabernacle reposed there, I saw it, by the influx of grace descending upon it from Mary and the co-operation of the whole heavenly court, increase in six until it became first a church and then a great shining city which slowly sank to the earth. I know not how it was, but I saw multitudes of living beings, first only their heads and then the whole figure, as if the earth on which they stood was drawing near to me and, at last, they were suddenly landed in the new Jerusalem, the new city which had descended upon the old Jerusalem, and which had now come upon earth. And here the vision ended.

★

On November 1st, she [Catherine Emmerich] said: "I have had an indescribably great and magnificent vision, but I cannot well express it. I saw an immense table with a red and white transparent cover. It was laden with all sorts of dishes. They were all like gold with blue letters around the rim. Flowers and fruits of every description lay there together, not broken from their stems, but living, growing, and though consumed, eternally renewed—the mere sight of them gave strength. (1) Bishops and all their clergy who had charge of souls appeared at the table as stewards and servers. Around it, seated on thrones or standing in half-circles were troops of saints in their choirs and orders. As I stood at the immense table, I thought the innumerable choirs around it were in one garden; but on looking more closely, I saw that each choir was in a separate garden and at a separate table. All received, however, a part of everything on the great table. And in all the gardens and fields and borders, the plants and branches and flowers were living as on the great table. The fruits were not eaten; they were received by a certain conscious perception. All the saints appeared with their various distinctive characteristics: many Bishops had little churches in their hands because they had built churches; and others, croziers, as they had only discharged their duties as pastors. By them were trees laden with fruits.

I wanted so badly to give some to the poor that I shook them. Quantities fell upon certain regions of the earth. I saw the saints in choirs according to their nature and strength, bringing materials to erect a throne at one end of the table, and all sorts of garlands, flowers and decorations for it. All was done with indescribable order as is proper to a nature exempt from defect, sin, and death; all seemed to spring forth spontaneously. In the meantime, spiritual guards watched over the table. Twenty-four old men now seated themselves on magnificent seats around the throne with harps and censers praising and offering incense. An apparition like an old man with a triple crown widespread mantle descended from on high upon the throne. In his forehead was a three-cornered light in which was a mirror which reflected everything: every one could see his own image therein.

From his mouth issued a beam of light in which were words. I distinguished letters and numbers quite distinctly, but I have now forgotten them. In front of his breast was a dazzlingly bright Crucified Youth from whose Wounds streamed forth arches of rainbow-colored light, which surrounded all the saints like a great ring, and with which their areolas mingled and played in unspeakable order, freedom, and beauty. From the luminous Wounds I saw a rain of many-colored drops fall upon the earth, like a shower of precious stones, each with its own meaning. I received then the knowledge of the value, virtue, secret properties and colors in general. I saw between the Crucified and the Eye in the forehead of the Old Man, the Holy Spirit under a winged form, and rays streaming to It from both. Before the Crucified, but a little lower down, was the Blessed Virgin surrounded by virgins. I saw a circle of Popes, Apostles, and virgins around the lower part of the cross. All these apparitions, as well as the myriads of saints and angels in circle after circle, were in constant movement mingling together in perfect unity and endless variety. The spectacle was infinitely richer and grander than of the starry heavens, and yet all was perfectly clear and distinct—but I cannot describe it!"

The youth took me to a place like the Heavenly Jerusalem, for it was all shining and transparent. We went to a great circular place surrounded by beautiful, sparkling palaces. In the centre stood a large table covered with dishes perfectly indescribable. From four of the palaces stretched arches of flowers which united above the table in a magnificent crown around which sparkled the holy names of Jesus and Mary. It was not a production of art, it was all alive and growing, each part producing fruit according to its kind, the arches formed of most varied flowers, fruits, and shining figures. I knew the signification of each and everyone, not only symbolically but as a substance, an essence which penetrated and enlightened the mind like sunbeams—but I cannot express it in words. On one side, a little beyond the palaces, stood two octagonal churches; one was Mary's the other the Christ-Child's. As I approached, there floated from all parts of the shining palaces, even through the walls, innumerable souls of descended children who came to bid me welcome. They appeared at first in the usual spiritual form but afterward they were shown to me as they were during life. I recognized several of my play-fellows long since dead.

St. Don Bosco

Born in 1815, Don Bosco was a priest, writer, and preacher. He was especially known for his ministry with the children of Turin , Italy. Although he was gifted with many prophecies and visions, it is his dreams that have established his legacy. One such dream was of Heaven called, *Hiking to Heaven*:

"Dream: Part One"

Since dreams come while sleeping, I, too, was

asleep. A few days ago, having to go out of town, I passed by the green-clad hills of Moncalieri. I was deeply impressed. Possibly this charming scene came back to my mind, stirring a desire to go hiking. As a matter of fact, that's what I decided to do in my dream.

I seemed to be with my boys in a vast plain which stretched out to a massively high hill. As we were all standing there, I suddenly proposed a hike.

"Yes, yes!" They all cheerfully shouted. Let's go!"

"Where to?" We asked one another undecidedly. While we looked hopefully at each other for suggestions, someone abruptly blurted out, "Let's hike to heaven."

"Yes, yes, to heaven!" The cry arose on all sides.

We started off, and after a while we reached the foot of the hill and began climbing. A magnificent view soon unfolded before our eyes. As far as we could see, the hillside was dotted with trees and saplings of all kinds—some small and tender, others tall and vigorous, none thicker than a man's arm. There were pears, apples, cherries, plums, vines, and other fruit trees. Amazingly, each tree had some flowers just blossoming and others in full bloom, some fruits just forming and others lusciously ripe. In other words, each tree showed the best of each season at one and the same time. The fruit was so plentiful that the branches sagged under its weight. Surprised at this phenomenon, the boys kept asking me for explanations. To satisfy their curiosity somewhat, I remember saying, "Well, it's like this. Heaven is not like our earth with its seasons. Its climate is always the same, embodying the best of every season. It is very mild and suitable for every tree and plant."

We stood entranced by the beauty surrounding us. The gentle breeze, the calm, and the fragrant air about us left no doubt that this climate was ideally suited to all kinds of fruits. Here and there, the boys were plucking apples, pears, cherries, or grapes while slowly climbing. When we finally reached the top of the hill, we thought we were in heaven, but in reality we were quite far from it.

From this vantage point we could see, beyond a vast plain, an extensive plateau and, in its center, a very lofty mountain soaring straight up to the clouds. Many people were determined, struggling up its steep sides, while on its summit stood One inviting and encouraging them to go up. We also spotted some persons descending from the top to help those who were too exhausted to continue the steep climb. Those reaching the top were greeted with vibrant cheers and jubilation. We understood that paradise was at the peak, and so we started downhill toward the plateau and mountain.

After covering a good part of the way—many boys were running far ahead of the crowd—we were in for quite a surprise. Some distance from the foot of the mountain the plateau held a big lake full of blood. Its length would extend from the Oratory to Piazza Castello. Its shore was littered with human limbs, fractured skulls, and remnants of corpses. It was a gruesome sight, a veritable carnage! The boys who had run on ahead stopped in their tracks, terrified. Being far behind and having no inkling of what was ahead, I was surprised to see them stop with horrified looks on their faces.

"What's wrong?" I shouted. "Why don't you keep going?"

"Come and see!" They replied. I hurried over and gazed upon the grim spectacle. As the others came up, they too took in the scene and immediately became silent and dispirited. Standing on the banks of that mysterious lake, I sought a way across, but in vain. Just in front of me, on the opposite bank, I could read a large inscription: *Through blood!*

Puzzled, the boys kept asking one another: "What does all this mean."

Then I asked someone (who he was I can't remember) for an explanation, and he replied, "This is the blood shed by the very many who have already reached the mountain's summit and are now in heaven. It is the blood of martyrs. Here, also, is the blood of Jesus Christ. In it were bathed the bodies of those who were martyred in testimony of the faith. No one may enter heaven without passing through this blood and being sprinkled by it. It guards the Holy Mountain—the Catholic Church. Whoever attempts to attack her shall drown in it. The torn limbs, mangled bodies, and broken skulls dotting the shore are the gruesome remains of those who chose to fight the Church. All have been crushed to bits; all have perished in this lake."

In the course of his explanation, the mysterious youth named many martyrs, including the papal soldiers who died defending the Pope's temporal power.

Then, pointing eastward to our right, he showed us an immense valley four or five times the size of the lake. "Do you see that valley?" He asked. "Into it shall flow the blood of those who will pass this way to scale this mountain—the blood of the just, of those who will die for the faith in days to come." Seeing that the boys were terrified by all they saw and heard, I tried to encourage them by saying that, if we were to die martyrs, our blood would flow into that valley, but our limbs would not be tossed about like those of the persecutors.

We then hastened to resume our march, skirting the shore of the lake. At our left stood the hill we had come down from; at our right were the lake and mountain. Where the lake ended, we saw a strip of land dotted with oaks, laurels, palms, and other trees. We went through it in search of a trail to the mountain, but only came across another vast lake. Floating in its waters were dismembered human limbs. On the shore stood an inscription: *Through water!*

"What does all this mean?" The boys again asked, mystified.

"This lake," someone replied, "holds the water which flowed from Christ's side. Small in quantity then, it has increased, is still increasing, and will keep increasing in the future. This is the baptismal water which washed and

purified those who climbed this mountain. In this same
water all who must still climb will have to be baptized and
purified. In it must be cleansed all those who want to go
to heaven. There is no other way to paradise than through
innocence or penance. No one can be saved without being
cleansed in this water." Then, pointing to the
dismembered limbs, he added, "These are the remains of
those who have recently attacked the Church."

      Meanwhile, a number of people and some of our
own boys, too, were swiftly darting across the lake,
skimming over the waters without wetting the soles of
their feet. We were astonished at this, but were told,
"These are the just. When the souls of the saints are freed
from their bodily prison or when their bodies are glorified,
they not only can tread lightly and swiftly over water, but
they can also fly through the air."

      Hearing this, all the boys, eager to cross the lake
like the other people, looked at me inquiringly. No one,
however, dared attempt it.

      "For my part, I don't dare," I replied. "It would be
rash to believe ourselves so just as to be able to cross the lake
without sinking."

      "If *you* don't dare, we dare even less," they all
exclaimed.

      Continuing on our way, always skirting the
mountain, we reached a third lake as large as the first, full of
flames and more torn human limbs. On the opposite shore
an inscription proclaimed: *Through fire!*

      While we were observing that fiery lake, that same
mysterious person spoke again and said, "This is the fire of
charity of God and His saints. These are the flames of love
and desire which all must pass if they have not gone through
blood and water. This is also the fire with which tyrants
tortured and consumed so many martyrs. Many are they
who had to go through it before climbing the mountain.
But these flames will also serve to reduce their enemies to
ashes."

      Thus for the third time we were seeing God's

enemies crushed and defeated.

Wasting no time, we advanced past the lake and came upon a fourth one, ever more frightening, shaped like a huge amphitheater. It was full of dogs, cats, wolves, bears, tigers, lions, panthers, snakes and other fierce monsters eager to pounce upon anyone within their reach. We saw people stepping over the heads of these raging beasts. We also saw boys fearlessly following them and suffering no injury.

I tried to call them back, shouting as loudly as I could: "Stop! Can't you see that those beasts are just waiting to devour you?" It was useless. They didn't hear me and kept treading upon the monsters' heads as if they were on firm, safe ground. My usual guide then said to me: "Those beasts symbolize the devils, the dangers and snares of the world. Those who step over them unharmed are the just, the innocent. Don't you know what Holy Scripture says?" 'You shall tread upon the asp and the viper; you shall trample down the lion and the dragon.' (Ps 91:13) It was of such souls that David spoke. And doesn't the Gospel say: '....I have given you power to tread on snakes and scorpions and all the forces of the enemy, and nothing shall ever injure you'" (Lk 10:19)?

We still kept asking one another: "How shall we cross over? Do we have to step over these wild beasts too?"

"Yes, let's go!" someone told me.

"I don't dare!" I replied. "It would be rash to believe ourselves so good as to be able to tread safely over these fierce beasts. Do as you wish, but not I."

"Then we won't try it either," the boys concluded.

We left that place and came upon a vast plain crowded with noiseless, earless, or headless people. Some, moreover, had no limbs, others had no hands or feet, and still others had no tongue or eyes. The boys were simply struck dumb at such an odd sight. A mysterious person explained: "These are God's friends. To save their souls, they have mortified their senses and performed good works. Many lost parts of their bodies in carrying out harsh penances or in working for God or their fellow men. The headless ones are those who is a special manner consecrated themselves to God."

While we were pondering these things, we could see that many people, having crossed the lake, were now ascending the mountain.

We also saw others, already at the top, helping and encouraging those who were going up, giving them joyous, hearty cheers of welcome as they reached the top. The handclapping and cheering woke me, and I found myself in bed. This ended the first part of the dream.

The following night, April 8ᵗʰ, Don Bosco again spoke to the boys, who couldn't wait to hear the continuation of the dream.

...Smiling upon their upturned faces, Don Bosco again spoke briefly paused and then went on thus:

"Dream: Part Two"

You will remember that at the bottom of a deep valley, near the first lake, stood another lake yet to be filled with blood. Well, after seeing all I have already described and going around that plateau, we found a passage taking us into another valley, which in turn opened into a large, wedge-shaped plaza. We entered it. Wide at the entrance, it gradually tapered into a trail at its other end and near the mountain. At this point the trail was wedged between two huge boulders so close together that only one person at a time could squeeze through. The plaza was filled with cheerful, happy people, all heading for the narrow mountain trail.

"Could that be the trail to heaven?" we asked one another. As the people reached it and squeezed through single-file, they had to pull their clothes right, hold their breath, and discard whatever they carried. This sufficed to convince me that surely this was the way to heaven, for I remembered that, to get there, one must not only rid himself of sin, but also give up all worldly ties and desires. "Nothing profane shall enter it," says the Apostle John.

CHAPTER SEVEN

THE QUEEN OF HEAVEN

Contemporary visionaries offer further insight into the Kingdom of Heaven. To a large extent, these insights are similar to the earlier ones. However, some have contributed greatly to our expanding understanding of Heaven. Such revelations are especially noted in accounts of the apparitions of the Virgin Mary, which have been quite numerous since the earth 19th century apparitions to St. Catherine Laboure at Ru Du Bac in Paris, France.

In 1830 at Ru due Bac, the Virgin Mary appeared three times to St. Catherine Laboure. In these apparitions, best known for the Miraculous Medal, Mary also spoke of Heaven. She revealed to St. Catherine that God was using her as the mediatrix of all graces between "Heaven and earth" and that "the saints in Heaven," especially her community's founder, St. Vincent de Paul, were "interceding before the throne of God for her and her community." Mary also confirmed in the final apparition that Heaven was moving towards a restoration with earth, a revelation best understood in the image of Mary given to St. Catherine for the medal. Theologians say the image confirmed that Mary was the woman of Genesis 3:15 and Revelations 12:1, two verses of Scripture known for their apocalyptic imagery.

Ru due Bac opened a new era of private revelation about Heaven. Not only were images of Paradise given to strengthen people's faith that Heaven existed, but the revelations also addressed the changing world, a world succumbing to evil. And this tendency toward sin was seriously affecting the eternal destination of souls in an unprecedented way. In essence, the revelations were more mature, reflecting God's presumption that Heaven was a well-accepted and proven article of the faith. But they cautioned that these dangerous times foretold in Scripture were making it increasingly difficult for souls to reach Heaven.

At La Salette, France, in 1846, Mary came to two young people—Melanie Calvat and Maximum Girard. No visions of Heaven were given to the children, but Mary again provided insight into Heaven. Her long, apocalyptic prophecy revealed how Heaven closely "directed all things on earth" and "responded" to the cries of the oppressed. This Church-approved apparition also communicated how God was planning to correct the injustices on earth to once again bring earth closer in line "with the way it is in Heaven." At La Salette, Mary spoke of efforts to "deny the existence of Heaven" and that she, as Mediatrix between Heaven and earth, would see that the prayers of the righteous were heard by God.

"The righteous will suffer greatly," said Mary at La Salette, "but their prayers, their penances and their tears will rise to Heaven"....."I call on the true disciples of the living God, who reigns in Heaven." Promising that the "fire of Heaven" would be sent to correct the world, Mary concluded her message at La Salette and departed "looking upwards to Heaven."

At Lourdes in 1858, Bernadette Soubirous also reported no visions of Heaven but she referred to Mary as the "Lady from Heaven." Similar to the apparitions at Ru de Bac and La Salette, Bernadette emphasized that Mary, "raised her eyes toward Heaven" before her March 25th, 1858 pronouncement that she was the " Immaculate Conception."

But perhaps the topic of Heaven is best understood from what Bernadette later revealed about her experiences. Bernadette said Mary once said to her. "I do not promise to make you happy in this world, but in the next." With this revelation, the importance of centering this life on the eternity of the next is emphasized—not just as a lesson for Bernadette, but for everyone. The message is clear: time allotted in this life is nothing but an opportunity to invest in the everlasting reality of the next. During her last days, Bernadette was said to be "homesick for Heaven." "Heaven, Heaven,." she kept murmuring. "They say there are some saints who did not go straight there because they had not longed for it enough," she added, "It won't be so in my case."

"You will soon be tasting the joys of Paradise," suggested her confessor Abbe Felivre as Bernadette was dying. "You'll be gazing on the beauty and glory of Our Lord, which the Blessed Mother gave you some idea of." "Oh how that does me good," Bernadette replied. On another day, the chaplain, finding Bernadette dejected, reminded her again of Heaven. "Be brave, sister," he said, "Remember Mary's promises. There's Heaven at the end." "Yes," Bernadette replied, "but the end is a long time coming. But the memory of it comforts me and turns my head to hope." Indeed, Bernadette was found to have written in her private notebook, "I will do everything for Heaven."

Many revelations over the late 19th and early 20th centuries continued to focus on the world to come in one way or another. Mary's Church-approved apparitions at Knock, Pellevoison, and Pontmain— all known for their overt symbolism of heaven—added to the theme of "Heaven shaping the events on earth to fulfill its plan." Likewise, the revelations at Pompeii, Italy, in 1875-76 emphasized Heavenly concepts, as Mary appeared to the visionaries sitting on a high throne, symbolizing her role as Queen of Heaven.

At Fatima in 1917, the powerful vision of Hell given to the three shepherd children illustrated the consequence of not attaining eternal life in Heaven. In one of her apparitions at Fatima, Mary promised Jacinta Marto, the youngest of the visionaries, that soon she would "go to Heaven." In urging chastity and the religious life, Jacinta once remarked, "I would enter a convent with great joy, but my joy is greater because I am going to Heaven." Similar statements were made by her brother and fellow visionary, Francisco, who died before he was ten, as the Virgin foretold.

Other 20th century visionaries and mystics have added to our understanding of Heaven. It would not be possible to examine them all, but some of the visions and revelations given to Sister Faustina Kowalska, Christina Gallagher, Georgette Faniel, Estela Ruiz, Father Stefano Gobbi, and the six visionaries at Medjugorje deserve attention.

Sister Maria Faustina Kowalska

The Diary of Sister Maria Faustina H. Kowalska, which expresses the complete record of the Divine Mercy Revelations, contains several powerful insights on Heaven. On May 12, 1935, Sister Faustina wrote of a vision related to Heaven:

In the evening, I just about got into bed, and I
fell asleep immediately. Though I fell asleep quickly; I
was awakened even more quickly. A little child came
and woke me up. The child seemed about a year old,
and I was surprised it could speak so well, as children of
that age either do not speak or speak very indistinctly.
The child was beautiful beyond words and resembled
the Child Jesus, and he said to me, **Look at the sky**.
And when I looked at the sky I saw the stars and the
moon shining. Then the child asked me, **Do you see
this moon and these stars?** When I said yes, he
spoke these words to me, **These stars are the souls
of faithful Christians, and the moon is the souls
of religious. Do you see how great the
difference is between the light of the moon and
the light of the stars? Such is the difference in
heaven between the soul of a religious and the
soul of a faithful Christian.** And he went on to say
that **True greatness is in loving God and in
humility**. (Diary 424)

In early 1936, Sister Faustina recorded another revelation
concerning Heaven:

I learned in the Heart of Jesus that in heaven
itself there is a heaven to which not all, but only chosen
souls, have access. Incomprehensible is the happiness in
which the soul will be immersed. O my God, oh, I
could describe this, even in some little degree. Souls are
penetrated by His divinity and pass from brightness to
brightness, an unchanging light, but never monotonous,
always new though never changing. O Holy Trinity,
make yourself known to souls! (Diary 592)

That same year, Jesus explained to Sister Faustina about the
glory reserved in Heaven for those who suffer like Christ:

At the same time, I saw a certain [Father

Sopocko] and, in part, the condition of his soul and the ordeals God was sending him. His sufferings were of the mind and in a form so acute that I pitied him and said to the Lord, "Why do you treat him like that?" And the Lord answered, **For the sake of his triple crown**. And the Lord also gave me to understand what unimaginable glory awaits the person who resembles the suffering Jesus here on earth. That person will resemble Jesus in His glory. The Heavenly Father will recognize and glorify our soul to the extent that He sees in us a resemblance to His Son. I understood that this assimilation into Jesus is granted to us while we are here on earth. I see pure and innocent souls upon whom God has exercised His justice; these souls are the victims who sustain the world and who fill up what is lacking in the Passion of Jesus. They are not many in number. I rejoice greatly that God has allowed me to know such souls. (Diary 604)

O Holy Trinity, Eternal God, I thank You for allowing me to know the greatness and the various degrees of glory to which souls attain. Oh, what a great difference of depth in the knowledge of God there is between one degree and another! Oh, if people could only know this! O my God, if I were thereby able to attain one more degree, I would gladly suffer all the torments of the martyrs put together. Truly, all those torments seem as nothing to me compared with the glory that is awaiting us for all eternity. O Lord, immerse my soul in the ocean of Your divinity and grant me the grace of knowing You; for the better I know You, the more I desire You, and the more my love for You grows. I feel in my soul an unfathomable abyss which only God can fill. I lose myself in Him as a drop does in the ocean. The Lord has inclined himself to my misery....my soul has become covered with verdure, flowers, and fruit, and has become a beautiful garden for His repose. (Diary 605)

Later that year (1936), Jesus explained to Sister Faustina how some souls actually begin to taste the delights of Heaven in this life:

> In that same moment, the soul drowns entirely in Him and experiences a happiness as great as that of the chosen ones in heaven. Although the chosen ones in heaven see God face to face and are completely and absolutely happy, still their knowledge of God is not the same. God has given me to understand this. This deeper knowledge begins here on earth, depending on the grace [given], but to a great extent it also depends on our faithfulness to that grace.
>
> However, the soul receiving this unprecedented grace of union with God cannot say that it sees God face to face, because even here there is a very thin veil of faith, but so very thin that the soul can say that it sees God and talks with Him. It is "divinized." God allows the soul to know how much He loves it, and the soul sees that better and holier souls than itself have not received this grace. Therefore, it is filled with holy amazement, which maintains its deep humility, and it steeps itself in its own nothingness and holy astonishment; and the more it humbles itself, the more closely God unites himself with it and descends to it. (Diary 771)

On November 27, 1936, Sister Faustina reported a vision of Heaven:

> Today I was in heaven, in spirit, and I saw its inconceivable beauties and the happiness that awaits us after death. I saw how all creatures give ceaseless praise and glory to God. I saw how great is happiness in God, which spreads to all creatures, making them happy; and then all the glory and praise which springs from this happiness returns to its source; and they enter into the depths of God, contemplating the inner life of God, the Father, the Son, and the Holy Spirit, whom they will never comprehend or fathom.

This source of happiness is unchanging in its essence, but it is always new, gushing forth happiness for all creatures. Now I understand Saint Paul, who said, "Eye has not seen, nor has ear heard, nor has it entered into the heart of man what God has prepared for those who love Him." (Diary 777)

And God has given me to understand that there is but one thing that is of infinite value in His eyes, and that is love of God; love, love and once again, love; and nothing can compare with a single act of pure love of God. Oh, with what inconceivable favors God gifts a soul that loves Him sincerely! Oh, how happy is the soul who already here on earth enjoys His special favors! And of such are the little and humble souls. (Diary 778)

The sight of this great majesty of God, which I came to understand more profoundly and which is worshiped by the heavenly spirits according to their degree of grace and the hierarchies into which they are divided, did not cause my soul to be stricken with terror or fear; no, no, not at all! My soul was filled with peace and love, and the more I come to know the greatness of God, the more joyful I become that He is as He is. And I rejoice immensely in His greatness and am delighted that I am so little because, since I am little, He carries Me in His arms and holds me close to His Heart. (Diary 779)

O my God, how I pity those people who do not believe in eternal life; how I pray for them that a ray of mercy would envelop them too, and that God would clasp them to His fatherly bosom. (Diary 780)

O Love, O Queen! Love knows no fear. It passes through all the choirs of angels that stand on guard before His throne. It will fear no one. It reaches God and is immersed in Him as in its sole treasure. The Cherubim who guards Paradise with Heavenly sword, has no power over it. O pure love of God, how great and unequaled you are. Oh, if souls only knew your power! (Diary 781)

In February 1938, another profound teaching on Heaven was given to Sister Faustina:

> When I had gone to the chapel for a moment, the Lord gave me to know that, among His chosen ones, there are some who are especially chosen, and whom He calls to a higher form of holiness, to exceptional union with Him. These are seraphic souls, from whom God demands greater love than He does from others. Although all live in the same convent, yet He sometimes demands of a particular soul a greater degree of love. Such a soul understands this call, because God makes this known to it interiorly, but the soul may either follow this call or not. It depends on the soul itself whether it is faithful to these touches of the Holy Spirit, or whether it resists them. I have learned that there is a place in purgatory where souls will pay their debt to God for transgressions. The soul which is specially marked by God will be distinguished everywhere, whether in heaven or in purgatory or in hell. In heaven, it will be distinguished from other souls by greater glory and radiance and deeper knowledge of God. In purgatory, by greater pain, because it knows God more profoundly and desires Him more vehemently. In hell, it will suffer more profoundly than other souls, because it knows more fully whom it has lost. This indelible mark of God's exclusive love, in the [soul], will not be obliterated. (Diary 1556)

That same year, Sister Faustina was again to understand more about God, His Holy Kingdom and what St. Paul meant when he said he could not describe Heaven:

> When, during adoration, I repeated the prayer, "Holy God," several times, a vivid presence of God suddenly swept over me, and I was caught up in spirit before the majesty of God. I saw how the Angels and the Saints of the Lord give glory to God. The glory of God is so great

that I dare not try to describe it, because I would not be able to do so, and souls might think that what I have written is all there is. Saint Paul, I understand now why you did not want to describe heaven, but only said that eye has not seen, nor ear heard, nor has it entered into the heart of man what God has prepared for those who love Him [cf. 1 Cor. 2:9; 2 Cor. 12:1-7]. Yes, that is indeed so. And all that has come forth from God returns to Him in the same way and gives Him perfect glory. Now I have seen the way in which I adore God; oh, how miserable it is! And what a tiny drop it is in comparison to that perfect heavenly glory. O my God, how good You are to accept my praise as well, and to turn Your Face to me with kindness and let me know that our prayer is pleasing to You. (Diary 1604)

Jesus also told Sister Faustina how, once in Heaven, all life's sufferings will be understood in His light:

When I met with the Lord, I said to Him "You are fooling me, Jesus: You show me the open gate of heaven, and again You leave me on earth." The Lord said to me, **When, in heaven, you see these present days, you will rejoice and will want to see as many of them as possible. I am not surprised, My daughter, that you cannot understand this now, because your heart is overflowing with pain and longing for Me. Your vigilance pleases Me. Let My word be enough for you; it will not be long now.**

And my soul found itself once again in exile. I lovingly united myself to the will of God, submitting myself to His gracious decrees. (Diary 783)

Christina Gallagher

Christina Gallagher is a 46 year-old woman from County Mayo, Ireland. Besides apparitions, Christina has reported many mystical experiences such as bilocation, visions, reading souls and the stigmata. Christina has reported both visions of Heaven as well as profound insights, granted her through infused knowledge. The following vision of Heaven occurred while she was praying the Stations of the Cross:

> While doing the Stations of the Cross, I became totally aware of seeing, with my eyes, a beam of light going up. Then I could see angels, and they were all like little babies. They were whiter than the light they were in. They ascended this beam of light, but they didn't fly up with their wings, although they had little wings. They seemed to move up the beam of light at will. At the top there was the most enormous area of white light. I've never seen anything like it.
>
> Then I saw a man sitting in a big wooden chair. This chair was very broad and powerful-looking. It was a chair of authority. This man Who sat in it had white hair. Although He looked old, there wasn't a line or a blemish in His face. He was very beautiful. His face was identical to Jesus,' only Jesus had brown hair and He had white hair, but Their faces were identical. When I saw them together, Jesus was on one side and the Blessed Mother was below Jesus on a step. I could see long steps, although they were nearly covered with light. And I remember saying that is my Eternal Father, that is Jesus His Son, and that's Our Blessed Mother. I thought, where is the Holy Spirit? I then became aware, that very moment, that all of the light I could see was the Holy Spirit. Now during all of this there were clouds, white clouds of light. There were different clouds with angels on each of them. They floated over where the Eternal Father was sitting and Jesus and His Blessed Mother were standing. I could hear millions of little voices mingled together. They were singing, but their singing sounded like music. It was beautiful. It sounded as if children were singing from a distance. I could hear a lot of children singing and their voices were coming across

as if on a breeze. It was like a beautiful sound from a distance, but it was softer, like music. I didn't know what they were singing, but it was so beautiful, all mingled together. It sounded so soft, like the wind itself, yet a beautiful sound came from it.

Christina also was shown how God draws individual souls to Himself in Heaven:

The soul, when it dies and it's purified for heaven according to the degree of its response to the Spirit and grace of God, will be drawn to an outer level of that Light of God in Heaven. It will be totally fulfilled according to the completion of its own capacity for God. To the extent of the decrease of self on earth, thereby permitting the increase of the Spirit of God, this capacity is increased in the souls who receive a high degree of God's calling in life. They will be drawn into the deeper areas of the Godhead. Such a soul could be described as a shining crystal allowing the Light of God to radiate or reflect through it, bringing greater glory to God.

Georgette Faniel

Georgette Faniel is an 84 year-old woman living in Montreal, Canada. She is a stigmatist, mystic, and victim soul who says she was once taken up into Heaven in a vision where she saw a host of wonders. The following interview is from the author's book, *Glory to the Father.*

Q. Have you seen Heaven?

A. *Not as such. Once during a prayer vigil, I was lifted up to heaven by a vision where I saw Jesus and Mary, along with many different people who were offering gifts to the Eternal Father. I was very sad because my hands were empty. Then I saw our Heavenly Mother come near me and ask me why I was crying. I told her that my hands were empty and that I couldn't return to earth to fill them with gifts for the Eternal Father. Mary told me:* **"I have a secret for you. Go and** *offer your heart filled with love to the Eternal Father and all will be well."* I did so after thanking her and awoke from the vision.

Q. Describe the people in Heaven.

A. *There were many people around as well as angels who were escorting Our Lady.*

Q. Can you tell me what the Celestial Court in Heaven has done for you?

A. *It helps me at the spiritual level. It accompanies me in my prayer especially at the time of the Eucharist during the offering. At the moment of the consecration, it prostrates itself and adores the thrice holy God.*

Q. Can you give me an example that could be verified when the Celestial Court helped you?

A. *When the Eternal Father asked me to kneel and to prostrate myself, I had the help of the Celestial Court. I have been an invalid for 32 years. This was an unwise move from the human point of view, but I made it in faith to obey the Eternal Father.*

Q. Georgette, we often forget the angels and the Celestial Court, don't we?

A. *Unfortunately, we have the tendency to forget the presence of our Guardian Angel and of the Celestial Court. Very often, the presence of our Guardian Angel is what protects us. We should invoke him and make him our confidant and our protector. It is comforting to know that he watches after us, that he sustains us in the hardships and that he will accompany us when God calls us to Himself.*

Q. Have you anything else to add?

A. *I advise you to have a very special devotion to Saint Michael the Archangel, and I would like the Church to resume the recitation of the prayer of Saint Michael the Archangel after Holy Mass. This would be a good protection for all of the Church.*

Q. Do you make a link between the Eucharist and the Celestial Court in Heaven?

A. *Yes, during the Holy Eucharist, the Eternal Father sometimes allows me to see the whole multitude of angels and saints in a state of adoration around the altar! This is an invitation to the respect and to the dignity which must be given to the celebrant and to the participants. An attitude of respect is absolutely necessary before the Real Presence. We too often forget this and we hurt the Lord by these acts of disrespect.*

Estela Ruiz

Estela Ruiz is a Mexican–American woman presently living in South Phoenix, Arizona. From December 1988 until December 1998, she reported apparitions of the Virgin Mary. Many of the messages she received contained references and insights into Heaven, including the following message of 17 August 1988:

THE JOYS OF HEAVEN

My Dear Children,

I come to pray with you this evening for the salvation of all men in the world. I also want to thank those who have committed to help me pray for your brothers and sisters. Your prayers are a very necessary part of my work. These are special times for all my children on earth and I come to be with you, as your heavenly Mother, to encourage all to move your lives in the direction of my Son.

These are days when you, my children, are celebrating the glory of my Assumption into Heaven, into the joy of being at my Son's side, at the feet of our Heavenly Father, and in constant praise of the Spirit of God. If you understand that I know the glorious joy of heaven, then you must surely understand why I cannot rest until all my earthly children have an opportunity to decide for God. On this joyous week, when my earthly children honor me, I beg all of you to make a decision to turn your lives totally to our Lord, so that one day we can all rejoice in praise of Him.

I beg you, my little ones, to open your hearts to my call. You are my children, and as your Mother I want to have you close to me for eternity. I want you to know the joy of loving God, in His goodness, in His mercy and in His love of you, as I know it.

These are days when I come to beg you to open your hearts to His love. I come to point out to you the secret to your joy and happiness. There is no human, no material object to your world that can give you the peace that you are seeking in your life. Nothing in your world can bring you the happiness that you were created to have. My Son died so that all of you could partake in His kingdom, glory and joy. Our Lord in His great mercy has opened the gates of His kingdom during these times so that all who desire may enter. But in order to enter, you must decide for God. He has left the decision to you. Listen to my words as I invite and encourage you to decide for Him.

I love you and thank you for listening to my words.

Father Stefano Gobbi

For 25 years (1973-1998), Father Stefano Gobbi of Italy reported receiving interior locutions from the Blessed Virgin Mary. Recognized by many Marian experts to be some of the most profound revelations of our time, Fr. Gobbi's messages from Mary have covered almost every theme, including the following messages:

LIVE IN PARADISE WITH ME

Live, my beloved sons, there where I am; in paradise, assumed body and soul, to share fully in the glory of my Son Jesus.

Always associated with Him through my role as Mother on this earth, I am now in paradise associated in the glory of the Son, who wants his Mother at his side, having given me a glorified body like his own.

Here is the reason for this extraordinary privilege of mine.

As by my *yes* I made it possible for the Word of God to assume his human nature in my virginal womb, so also by my *yes* I entrusted myself to the action of my Son Jesus, who assumed your Mother into the glory of heaven, body and soul.

Mine is a transfigured and glorified body, but a real body, my beloved sons. Mother and Son are now together in paradise forever.

But I am also your real Mother; and thus I can love you not only with my soul, but also with my glorified body.

I love you with this Mother's heart of mine which has never ceased to beat with love for you.

Beloved sons, you also should be living there where I am: *live in paradise with me.*

It is true, you are still on this earth of sorrows and often you experience all its weight and suffering.

But why, while still living in this land of exile, do you not also live, even now, there where your Mother is? Live in paradise with me and do not let yourselves be attracted by the world, nor imprisoned by this earth.

Today there is a tendency which is extremely false and dangerous. That of looking only at this earth. It is as though we are afraid that, if we look at paradise, we will be drawn away from the duties of daily life. Live in paradise with me, and then you will live well, even on this earth!

Carry out here below the plan of the heavenly Father and you will create true happiness all about you.

The more you look to the Father and live with me, the more will you labor on this earth for you own good and the good of all.

Paradise—that is, the real one—can never be found on this earth.

How he deceived and seduces you, this Adversary of mine who in his fury tries to prevent you from coming up here to be with my Son and with me!

Paradise is found only in the light of the Most Holy Trinity, with my Son Jesus and with me.

The angels and the saints are illumined by this light and they rejoice in it. All paradise is resplendent with his light.

Live then while searching for, cherishing and gazing upon this paradise which awaits you, my beloved sons.

And here below, *live in the paradise of my Immaculate Heart*.

Then you will be serene and deeply happy.

You will always be littler and more abandoned, poorer and more chaste.

And the littler, poorer and more chaste you become, the more you will be able to enter into the paradise of my Immaculate Heart, where time is now marked by the beating of a heart which knows no stopping (August 15, 1976).

★

THE COMMUNION OF SAINTS

I am the Queen of all the Saints. Today you are bid to lift up your eyes here to paradise, where so many of your brothers have preceded you. They are praying for you and helping you, that that reign of Jesus, which in heaven is the cause of our joy and glory, may soon come also upon earth.

May this living communion with all your brothers who are already in paradise become ever more intense. The communion of the saints must be lived out still more fully at these times, because there is only one Church in which my Son Jesus lives and reigns and is glorified by his brethren, who are still struggling, or suffering, or rejoicing in eternal beatitude.

As you go about, bringing my invitation everywhere and gathering my children into my cohort, how greatly you are assisted, protected and defended by your brothers who have already arrived up here!

They form a crown of light about my Immaculate Heart. Each one of these lights is reflected on each of you, and illumines and guides you on your journey.

Your heavenly Mother wants to strengthen the bonds of love which unite you to heaven, so that you may daily benefit from the communion of the saints, and go forward united with them (Nov. 1, 1981).

★

YOUR PLACE IN PARADISE

Today, look at those who have already gone before you into glory. Round about my Immaculate Heart, they form a luminous crown of love, of joy and of glory.

This is also your place in paradise. It is being prepared for all of you who listen to my voice, who consecrate yourselves to my Immaculate Heart, live in filial dependence upon me and offer yourselves completely for the perfect fulfillment of my plan. You are, here below, my dearly beloved children. You are my apostles, called to spread everywhere the light of my motherly presence and to point out of all the road that they have need to follow in order to reach Christ, from whom alone can come the new era of holiness, of justice, and of peace.

For this reason, feel at your side, each day, the saints and the blessed of heaven; call upon them for help and protection. Feel also at your side the souls of the just, who are still suffering and praying in purgatory, awaiting the moment of their full beatitude in the perfect contemplation of the Lord. With you they form one single cohort, under my orders. For all, I am the Mother and the Queen. Each one has an irreplaceable part to play in my victorious plan.

In these times, I want to make deeper, stronger

and more extraordinary your communion with those
who have preceded you in the earthly life and now
enjoy eternal salvation. As a motherly gift of my
Immaculate Heart, I offer you, as a precious help, the
souls of the saints in paradise and of the just in purgatory.
You are being exposed to grave dangers and they can
assist you in overcoming them. You are victims of the
subtle snares of my Adversary and they can give you
light that you may be able to see them, and strength that
you may flee from them. You are fragile and weak and
often happen to fall again into sin; they can always lead
you a hand to walk along the road of good and of
holiness.

Travel, therefore, together with them, along
the road which I have traced out for you together, I am
leading you to peace.

Peace will come to you from my Immaculate
Heart when this, your communion of life, of love and of
joy will have then been perfectly accomplished (Nov.
1, 1986).

★

AT THE HOUR OF YOUR DEATH

Beloved sons, today you are gathered together
in prayer, as you call to mind your brothers who have
gone before you in the sign of faith and now sleeping the
sleep of peace.

How great is the number of my beloved ones
and children consecrated to my Immaculate Heart, who
have now entered into the repose of the Lord!

Many of them are sharing in the fullness of joy,
in the perfect possession of God and, together with the
angelic cohorts, are lights which shine in the eternal
blessedness of paradise.

Many are in purgatory, with the certainty of
having been saved forever, although still in suffering of

purification, because their possession of God is not yet full and perfect.

Today I want to tell you that these brothers of yours are especially close to you and form the most precious part of my victorious cohort. I have but one single cohort, just as my Church is one and one alone, united in the joyous experience of the communion of saints.

The saints intercede for you, light up your path, assist you with their most pure love, defend you from the subtle snares which my Adversary sets for you, and anxiously await the moment of your meeting.

The souls who are being purified pray for you, offer their sufferings for your well-being and, through your prayers, they are assisted in being set free from entering into the eternal joy of paradise.

Those saints who, while on earth, had lived the consecration to my Immaculate Heart, making up a crown of love to alleviate the sorrows of your heavenly Mother, form here above my most beautiful crown of glory. They are close to my throne and follow your heavenly Mother wherever she goes.

Those souls in purgatory who, while on earth, had formed part of my cohort, now enjoy a special union with me, feel in a special way my presence which sweetens the bitterness of their suffering, and shortens the time of their purification. And it is I myself who go to receive these souls into my arms, that I many lead them into the incomparable light of paradise.

Thus I am always close to all of you, my beloved ones and children consecrated to my Heart, during your painful earthly pilgrimage, but I am close to you in a most special way *at the hour of your death*.

How many times, as you recite the holy rosary, have you repeated this prayer to me: "Holy Mary, Mother of God, pray for us sinners, now and *at the hour of our death!*" This is an invocation which I listen to with great joy, and it is always heard by me. If, as Mother, I am close to each one of my children at the hour of death, I am especially close to you who, through your consecration, have always lived in the secure refuge of my Immaculate Heart.

At the hour of your death, I am close to you, with the splendor of my glorified body, I receive your souls into my motherly arms, and I bring them before my Son Jesus, for his particular judgement.

Think of how joyful must be the meeting of Jesus with those souls who are presented to Him by his very own Mother! This is because I cover them with my beauty, I give them the perfume of my holiness, the innocence of my purity, the white robe of my charity and, where there remains some stain, I run my motherly hand over it to wipe it away and to give you that brightness which makes it possible for you to enter into the eternal happiness of paradise.

Blessed are those who die close to your heavenly Mother. Yes, blessed, because they die in the Lord, they will find rest from their labors, and their good deeds will follow them.

My beloved ones and children consecrated to my Immaculate Heart, today I invite you to enter into a great intimacy with me during your life, if you wish to experience the great joy of seeing me close to you and of welcoming your souls into my motherly arms, *at the hour of your death* (Nov. 2, 1992).

★

LOOK UP TO HEAVEN

Live today with me, beloved sons, in paradise where I was assumed with my soul and my body, to participate in a perfect manner in the glory of my Son Jesus.

— *Look up to heaven.* Your heavenly Mother was assumed into heaven, at the very moment when she closed her eyes to her earthly life. And then, surrounded by a multitude of the angelic host, who exalted and venerate me as Queen. I was raised up to the glory of paradise.

— The Most Holy Trinity has bowed down, delighted and glorified, and in me has reflected the rays of its eternal and divine splendor My Son Jesus, who had already ascended into heaven to take his seat at the right hand of the Father, has welcomed me with filial love and joy, and has wanted me at this side, to share in his royal power in subjecting all things to Himself.

— Thus have I become Queen, because the Most Holy Trinity has confirmed me in my glorious role of beloved Daughter of the Father, Mother of the Son, and the Spouse of the Holy Spirit.

— *Look up to heaven.* In paradise, I exercise fully my maternal power. As Mother, I am close to Jesus in order to intercede for you. I cause to descend from my Immaculate Heart the graces of which you have need, in order to walk with me along the painful road of these last times. Thus you also can arrive here in paradise, where with Jesus, your heavenly Mother awaits you.

I am close to Jesus, to offer my motherly work of reparation to the Most Holy and Divine Trinity. For this, I gather in the chalice of my Immaculate Heart all your sufferings, the great sorrows of all humanity in the time of its great tribulation and I present them to Jesus, as a sign of reparation for all the sins which are committed each day in the world.

And thus I have again succeeded in postponing the time of the chastisement decreed by Divine Justice, for a humanity which has become worse than at the time of the flood.

— *Look up to heaven.* From heaven, you will see my Son Jesus returning on the clouds, in the splendors of his divine glory. Then finally the triumph of my Immaculate Heart in the world will be accomplished.

To prepare for this divine prodigy, I want to

establish my motherly triumph in the hearts and the souls of all my children. For this, I have caused my Marian Movement of Priests to spring up within the Church, and I have brought my little son to every part of the world and, in him and by means of him, I have manifested myself to all. For this reason, I continue to ask him to go to remote and distant places, in order to help you enter, through your consecration, into the safe refuge of my Immaculate Heart.

Thus you too, with your soul and heart, are living in paradise where I dwell, even if with your bodies you are still dwelling on this earth. In this way you too share in my maternal glory. And thus you too unite yourselves in my work of intercession and reparation, and prepare, in prayer, in silence and in suffering, for the awaited moment—so hoped for—for the triumph of my Immaculate Heart, in the greatest and most glorious triumph of my Son Jesus.

Medjugorje

On June 24, 1981, six Croatian children in the village of Medjugorje, Hercegovina, reported that the Blessed Virgin Mary appeared to them on a small hill named Podbrdo. Since then, the apparitions have continued, with three of the visionaries still reporting daily visitations (as of March 2000).

From the beginning, the messages of the Virgin Mary at Medjugorje have called the faithful to focus on the eternal life ahead and have stressed that the world will go through such a period of change in the near future that every soul needs to be prepared for what afterlife could bring them. All six visionaries at Medjugorje report they have seen Heaven. Here are their exact words on Heaven, as excerpted from several interviews:

Jacov Colo is the youngest of the six visionaries and received his last daily apparition in 1998. In Janice T. Connell's book, *Queen of the Cosmos,* he reveals what he saw and learned about Heaven:

Q. Jacov, you have been visited every day of your life since you were ten the Mother of God. How do you relate to her?

A. *It is very hard to find the words to describe this relationship we have. I am her child, and I am a messenger of God's plan. She has explained to me that she is the mother of all people on the earth, not just me. She is available to each person on the earth. Anyone who wants, can have the Blessed Mother as his Mother, to guide him and protect him on earth and bring him home to Heaven.*

Q. Do you know much about your own future, Jacov?

A. *The Blessed Mother has taught me many things.*

Q. *Do you know whether you will go to Heaven when you die?*

A. I have been in Heaven already.

Q. *Is it hard to live on the earth after you have been in Heaven?*

A. *I would not like to talk about my suffering.*

Q. Will you tell us about Heaven?

A. *When you get there, then you will see how it is.*

Q. You have said that the reason the Blessed Mother took you there was to show you what it would be like for those who remain faithful to God—would you tell us any more?

A. *If I thought about it too much, I would die of loneliness.*

In Connell's second book on Medjugorje, *The Visions of the Children,* the author explains more about Jacov's background and heavenly experiences:

> Jacov is an orphan. He was the only child of a father who abandoned the family when he was eight years-old. His mother, who had suffered from alcoholism, died when he was twelve. He has been told by the Blessed Mother that his mother is with her in Heaven.
>
> Is Jacov sensitive? Imagine for a moment the relationship with the unseen world we have only heard or read about, that Jacov Colo experiences daily. He has been inside the place known as heaven. The memory is powerful for him.

Q. Tell us about the things of heaven, Jacov.

A. *There really are no words.*

Q. Jacov, the philosophers and theologians have written many things about heaven. Do you know about philosophers and theologians?

A. *I am a single man. I have seen some of the books that speak about the things of heaven.*

Q. What do you think of the books?

A. *They have a lot of words in them.*

Q. Are the words correct?

A. *It is tedious to work through all the words. If that were my avenue to heaven, I might have no understanding at all [laughter].*

Q. Tell us your understanding of heaven.

A. *I have been there. It is difficult for me to talk about it.*

Q. Is it difficult to live on earth once you have been in heaven?

A. *That is an understatement.*

Q. Jacov, you said that if you thought about heaven too much, you would die of loneliness. How do you handle the memories of heaven, hell, and purgatory?

A. *The Blessed Mother asks us to be careful of the problem of the tyranny of memories.*

Q. What does that mean?

A. *She asks us to trust God's love to make all things well. She asks us to surrender the past to her maternal care and to remember only in the light of God's love.*

Q. Does that mean you do not dwell on the past?

A. *I try not to even think of the past or the future. The Blessed Mother has taught me that I have enough to do just today.*

Q. Do you know whether you will go to heaven when you die?

A. *For me the path is most difficult.*

Q. In what way?

A. *I have been chosen to be a messenger of this apparition. I do not want to disobey God. My path is difficult.*

Ivan Dragecivic, the only other male visionary at Medjugorje, has also seen Heaven. The following interview is excerpted from Janice T. Connell's, *Queen of the Cosmos:*

Q. Do you know whether you're going to Heaven when you die, Ivan?

A. *I have seen Heaven already.*

Q. Will you tell us about it?

A. *Heaven is worth any cost! Jesus showed us that, with His death on the Cross. His death was not the end. He rose from the dead, glorified, to put an end to death forever for God's children. People in heaven are happy. They live in the fullness of God.*

Q. Can you explain what that means?

A. *You'll have to experience it to know. It is better than anything you can imagine!*

Maria Pavlovic Lunetti was chosen by the Virgin Mary to be the recipient of Mary's monthly message to the world. The following interview is excerpted from Fr. Réne Laurentin and Fr. Ljudevit Rupcic's book, *Is The Virgin Mary Appearing at Medjugorje:*

Q. Have you seen anything else besides Our Lady and Jesus?

A. *We saw heaven, hell, and purgatory. Our Lady showed us this also. Once, here at Vicka's house, once at my house, and another time, but I don't remember where. I saw heaven, like people who were so happy. No, I can't describe that beauty. In fact, you see that the love of God is there.*

Ivanka Ivankovic Elez was the second of the visionaries to no longer see Mary on a daily basis. The following interview is from Janice T. Connell's *Queen of the Cosmos:*

Q. Did you see Heaven, Hell, and Purgatory, Ivanka?

A. *I saw Purgatory and Heaven as a picture. I told the Blessed Mother I did not want to see Hell.*

Q. What did Heaven look like?

A. *It is a place that is very, very beautiful. Most beautiful.*

Q. Were there houses in Heaven?

A. *None that I saw.*

Q. Were there trees?

A. *No, I saw only people.*

Q. Did they have *bodies?*

A. *Yes,* they did.

Q. What did they wear?

A. *I saw them in gray robes.*

Q. Were they happy?

A. *Everyone* I saw was filled with a happiness I can't explain—and I can't forget!

Q. Do you long for that happiness yourself?

A. *I know some of that happiness when I am with the Blessed Mother, and when I pray.*

In Connell's book *The Visions of the Children*, Ivanka reveals more about Heaven:

Q. Do you know what humility is, Ivanka?

A. *It is part of the things of heaven.*

Q. You have seen heaven, haven't you?

A. *Yes.*

Q. Can you explain heaven?

A. *Words can never describe heaven. Those who love God know about heaven. Those who do not love God yet must pray. In that way all can understand and long for heaven.*

Mirjana Dragecivic Soldo is the oldest of all the visionaries and has also seen Heaven. As with the other visionaries, Connell asked her about Heaven in her book, *The Visions of the Children*:

Q. You have seen heaven?

A. *Yes.*

Q. Did you experience heaven with your heart, or did you really see it with your eyes?

A. *I saw heaven with my eyes.*

Q. What did you see?

A. *Heaven was like a video unfolding before my eyes. I saw happy, healthy people, both men and women. The grass was of a beauty I can't describe. The flowers were so beautiful I can't describe them.*

Q. Why did the Blessed Mother want you to see heaven?

A. *She told me many people on earth today do not believe heaven exists. She said God has chosen us six visionaries to be instruments of His love and mercy. I have personally seen heaven. It exists! I've seen it! Those who stay faithful to God to the end will see heaven as a reward for their faithfulness.*

In her book, *Visions of the Children,* Connell writes specifically about **Vicka Ivankovic's** heavenly experiences:

> She [Vicka] knows much about the unseen world. She has been to heaven. She describes heaven as a place that is not beyond the horizon. She says it is not tomorrow. Vicka says heaven is all around us, and indeed within us, even on earth, for those who live right in the center of God's will—those who experience an awareness of God's presence, in effect, experience the presence of God in all that is. Though Vicka says the experience is not constant on earth as it is in heaven, she claims that, for those who really know God, heaven is possible to experience while still on earth. All this is the fruit of God's love, His grace, His mercy, she says.

> Vicka describes heaven as a vast place; conceptually, she says, it is "unlimited" and, given the language and education barrier, she may have been attempting to explain that heaven is in some way infinite, because God is infinite, and heaven is a union with God in all that is. She describes people, very happy people. They were dressed, she says daily to those who ask, in pink, gray, and yellow robes. "They are so happy. You can see it on their faces."

> "What kind of happiness? someone asks.

"*They are full,*" she responds.

"What does that mean?"

"*Well,*" Vicka volunteers, "*the Blessed Mother said, 'See how happy they are. And they know they deserve it.'*"

Vicka speaks of a great light that is in heaven. "*Is it a physical light, like the light from the sun? Or is it light that floods the intellect to illumine all those mysteries that have been hidden throughout the ages?*"

It is even more than that, she says. "*There are no mere words to describe heaven. You just have to experience it.*" Heaven is a reward for those who stay faithful to God until the end, she says. Vicka announces that when our body dies, nothing changes for us except that we no longer have a body. We are exactly the same person, she says, except the physical body is gone. Also we no longer have free will. We must now face, in God's light, all the results of our free choices, which we made while we had a body. We now can see, she says, the results of our choices until the end of time. We can't remedy anything now. We are totally dependent upon God's mercy and the love and kindness of those still on earth to repair and restore any harm we have done to any person, place, or thing on earth.

You have been in heaven, Vicka. What is it like? You have described flowers, trees, people in yellow, pink, and gray robes.

"*The Blessed Mother took Jacov and me to heaven. It is a kingdom of love, of joy, of peace. God made every child of His to live in that kingdom. It is sin that keeps us out.*"

You have told us that some people are able to experience heaven while on earth through obedience to God's will. You said that those who do God's will have love and peace and joy even in the midst of great suffering.

"*Yes. It is sin that interrupts love. It is sin that destroys peace. It is sin that kills joy.*"

★

While the apparitions and revelations of the Virgin Mary over the centuries have certainly continued and, for that matter, magnified the reality of the existence of Heaven, it is perhaps in some of the divine and mystical gifts the Virgin has left at the sites of her interventions that we are especially made aware of the importance of keeping our lives aimed at obtaining Paradise.

These gifts have been the Brown Scapular, the Rosary and other devotions or sacramentals. With many of them, Mary revealed promises related to helping a soul "get to Heaven." Let us take a brief look at some of these divine favors.

THE SCAPULAR

In the thirteenth century, Saint Simon Stock received the Brown Scapular from the Virgin Mary in an apparition. With it came the promise of Heaven for all who are wearing it at the time of their death. "Whoever dies clothed in this habit shall not suffer the fires of Hell," Mary told Saint Simon as she presented the Scapular to him. The "Promise," as it is known, meant the certainty of Heaven. However, it must be noted that it did not mean one could die in serious sin and still be saved, even if unrepentant. Rather, it meant that souls who wear the Scapular will receive the graces necessary to not die in mortal sin. Great saints, such as St. Robert Bellarmine, have said that the "promise" refers to the "grace of perseverance in the state of grace" or the "grace of a final contrition."

A second heavenly promise attached to the wearing of the Scapular is the Sabbatine Privilege. This divine promise, which Pope Pius XI said "is the greatest of all privileges of the Mother of God, extending even after death," involves the heavenly assurance that those who die wearing the Brown Scapular, and fulfill two other conditions, will be freed from Purgatory into Heaven on the first Saturday after death. The other two conditions involve chastity, according to one's state of life, and the daily praying of the Office. (The keeping of fasts has been substituted as a condition).

The Sabbatine Privilege, once again, is said to have also originated through the intercession of the Virgin Mary in a 14th century

Inside Heaven and Hell

apparition to Pope John XXII.

THE ROSARY

Like the Scapular, faithful recitation of the Rosary is said to offer a soul many divine promises, all of which are directly or indirectly related to getting to Heaven. There are fifteen promises of Mary to Christians who recite the Rosary. Here are just several which are associated with Heaven:

1. It will cause virtue and good works to flourish; it will obtain for souls the abundant mercy of God; it will withdraw the hearts of men from the love of the world and its vanities, and will lift them to the desire of eternal things.

2. The soul which recommends itself to Mary by the recitation of the Rosary, shall not perish.

3. Whoever shall recite the Rosary devoutly, applying himself to the consideration of its sacred mysteries, shall never be conquered by misfortune. God will not chastise him in His justice, he shall not perish by an unprovided death; if he be just he shall remain in the grace of God, and become worthy of eternal life.

4. Those who are faithful to recite the Rosary shall have during their life and at their death the light of God and the plenitude of His graces; at the moment of death they shall participate in the merits of the Saints in Paradise.

5. The faithful children of the Rosary shall merit a high degree of glory in Heaven.

6. Devotion to the Rosary is a great sign of predestination (for Heaven).

THE NINE FIRST FRIDAYS DEVOTION

In the seventeenth century, Jesus appeared to St. Margaret Mary Alacoque at the convent at Parlay Le Monial in Burgundy, France. St. Margaret Mary received from Him the Sacred Heart Devotion, which taught the means of acquiring "perfect love" of Jesus Christ and tender devotion to His Sacred Heart. Specifically, the devotion involves attending Mass and receiving Holy Communion on the first Friday of the month for nine consecutive months in reparation for those who do not receive or love Christ, or who wound Him. The promise attached to this devotion is none other than the "assurance" of the graces necessary to get to Heaven.

THE FIVE FIRST SATURDAYS DEVOTION

At Fatima in 1917, the Virgin Mary told the three visionaries that Heaven desired the Communion of Reparation of First Saturdays from the faithful. This meant that the people, if they choose to, could do the following devotion on the first Saturday for five consecutive months.

1. Pray the Rosary

2. Wear the Scapular

3. Make the Communion of Reparation. This included Confession, Communion, the Rosary, and to spend at least 15 minutes in meditation upon the mysteries of the Rosary.

Upon completion, Mary promised "I will assist at the hour of death with all the graces that are needed." Simply defined, Mary promised a soul would not die in sin and thus, was assured to go to Heaven.

There have been many other devotions with promises of graces to help a soul "get to Heaven." These devotions are special, some of which are the Two Hearts Scapular, the Red Scapular, the Green Scapular, the Hour of Great Mercy Devotion, the Stations of the Cross, the Crown of Thorns Prayer, the Holy Wounds Devotion, the Seven Dolars of The Blessed Virgin Mary Devotion, the Three Hail Marys Prayer, the Two Divine Promises and many more.

CHAPTER EIGHT

THE BEATIFIC VISION

Today, most Catholics regard Heaven as the place and condition of supreme beatitude. Why is it considered both a place and a condition?

It is a place, theologians say, because God created human "bodies." Earthly bodies have material substances and resurrected bodies have some form of material substance, as reported in Scripture and mystical accounts. Though the resurrected or transformed body may occupy space in a way unknown to us, bodies—in general—need a "place" in which to exist. The significance of this as it relates to Heaven is evident: Jesus and Mary had earthly bodies that are now, the Church teaches, in Heaven. Likewise, according to Church teachings, all souls at the General Resurrection will have their bodies restored to them and will then be assigned to Heaven or Hell. Therefore, while Heaven's location is not established, Divine Revelation does not permit us to ignore its existence.

However, Heaven is not only a place but a condition or state of being. This doctrine of faith involves what Pope Benedict XII refers to as the "divine essence":

> The souls of all the saints are in heaven before the resurrection of the body and the general judgement. They see the divine essence by a vision which is intuitive and facial without the intermediation of any creature in that view. By this vision they enjoy the divine essence, they are truly blessed, they have eternal life and repose.

The Council of Florence established that souls in the state of grace, after being purified, enter into Heaven, see the Triune God as He truly is, but with a degree more or less perfect, according to "the diversity of their merits."

Garrigou Lagrange, a 20th century theologian, points to the witness of Tradition in establishing this teaching:

> The existence of the beatific vision is affirmed in clear and explicit fashion by the Fathers of the apostolic age. St. Ignatius is penetrated by this thought, the possession of God in pure light. St. Polycarp expects the recompense promised to the martyrs, namely, reunion with Christ at the right hand of God. It is true that the millenaristic error is accepted by St. Justin and Tertullian, since they think that the entrance of the just into the kingdom of heaven will be restarted until the time of the general resurrection of the last judgment. Nevertheless, these early writers defend the existence of heaven, even the most millenaristic among them. And many of these early Fathers affirm that the souls of the martyrs enjoy the possession of God immediately after death, before the general resurrection.
>
> In the 4th century this doctrine is the one commonly received. Among the ante-Nicean Fathers who most firmly declare the existence of the beatific vision, we must signalize St. Irenaeus. He writes: "That which God gives to those who love Him is the gift of seeing Him, as the prophets have announced. Man of himself cannot see God, but God wills to be seen by us and He grants to us what He wills, when He wills and as He wills." St. Hippolytus speaks in the same manner.
>
> Clement of Alexandria and Origen also believed that a clear vision of God was reserved for the elect by grace of Christ. St. John Chrysostom is specific, but he repeats the words of St. Paul: "We see now through a glass in a dark manner, but then face to face."
>
> St. Cyprian writes: "What glory and what joy to be admitted to see God, to be honored with Christ our

Lord! This is the joy of salvation, this is eternal life: to live with the just, with all the friends of God in the kingdom of immorality. When God shall shine upon us we will rejoice with inexpressible gladness, sharing forever the kingdom of Christ."

St. Augustine often emphasizes the thought that all the saints in heaven, like the angels, rejoice with Christ in the vision of God.

Fr. Lagrange argues that, contrary to heretical teaching which says no human could ever see God without a medium, seeing God will be a supernatural vision and that through reason we can understand this doctrine. Like miracles, says Fr. Lagrange, the beatific vision is supernatural in its very essence. Therefore, belief in Heaven is a spiritual reality that once accepted, takes on the nature of a place and an experience understandable through our earthly experiences and our ability to reason with the help of grace.

So what does all of this mean for a Catholic?

For a Catholic, belief in Heaven involves faith that Heaven really exists, that it is a spiritual kingdom souls can behold with their bodily eyes—after death and later after the Last Judgment. It is a visible kingdom superior to anything else, a place where the blessed of God dwell and contemplate Him. In addition to the place and condition of Heaven, we might also consider some of it's notable attributes, such as beauty, brightness, size, and makeup.

Heaven's beauty, according to the saints, is indescribable. It is beyond anything that we can conceive of or relate to in our earthly experience or our imaginations. The light of Heaven has been described as a consuming brilliance that penetrates the vast space of Heaven—a breathtaking expanse that has been depicted as immeasurable. Mansions and castles are spoken of, perhaps only symbolically, but the Church teaches that each soul will have his/her dwelling place.

Interestingly, Heaven has been described in both pastoral and urban terms—both are acceptable Church teachings. But most of all it is considered as the Presence of God. Many of the proposed details of Heaven, whether pastoral or urban, appeal to the human senses of taste, touch, sight, smell, and hearing. These sensory details, supported by saints such as Augustine and Anselm, are often associated with conceptions of an earthly paradise.

A sacred society is said to exist in Heaven, where the blessed converse and inherently recognize Divine order and authority. Wisdom and love, not fear, guide their understanding. In fact, the blessed of Heaven enjoy a fellowship of mutual happiness, as they all share in the inheritance of God.. Each soul has attributes which, although they may vary, have been endowed for the glory of God. In Heaven, the children of God are like countless stars moving around the light and warmth of the sun.

Besides their beauty, each soul in Heaven is to be endowed with impassibility, agility, and subtlety. Glorified bodies, then, will be impervious to injury, traveling great distances at the speed of thought and able to pass through all matter. Bodies will also be invisible or visible at will. Many other inestimable gifts are to be granted to each individual soul.

Despite these super-human abilities, St. Anselm was of the opinion that souls would still have sensory capabilities, allowing souls to see indescribable beauty, to hear incredible hymns of praise, to smell the delicious odors of paradise, to taste its sweet substances, and to experience wondrous, pleasurable sensations.

Likewise, it is believed that conversation in Heaven will be exceedingly pleasurable, filled with affection and love and boundless charity. The blessed will share in the triumph of each other's earthly lives. Gratitude will especially abound for those who helped others to get to Heaven. The bliss of Heaven will provide fertile ground for heartfelt affection and extreme kindness, as well as ecstasies and divine consolations

In Heaven, creation in the light of God, will be experienced and understood. The states of intellect, memory, will, imagination, and understanding will be perfected in the blessed. Each soul will be endowed with the wisdom of God , and the powers of the universe will be revealed. Nothing will be hidden or mysterious, and clear insight will be granted. Most of all, the love of God for His people and His people for Him will exist in its fullest perfection. Indeed, the love of Heaven will be the joy above all joys.

Finally, in trying to understand the meaning of the beatific vision, we must realize that Heaven is not merely the gazing upon God, but a true intimate union with Him. We shall retain, however, our personality and human nature—but in a perfected way. As St. Thomas Aquinas said, "The glory of Heaven does not destroy nature, but perfects it."

Therefore, a world of beauty and perfection, a new order, will be in place, one that provides a life of peace, rest, intellectual pleasure, love, and perfect enjoyment. No unhappiness will find its way into the abode of the blessed. With the words of Pope John Paul II, let us conclude our look at Heaven:

> When the form of this world has passed away, those who have welcomed God into their lives and have sincerely opened themselves to his love, at least at the moment of death, will enjoy that fullness of communion with God which is the goal of human life.
>
> As the *Catechism of the Catholic Church* teaches, "this perfect life with the Most Holy Trinity, this communion of life and love with the Trinity, with the Virgin Mary, the angels and all the blessed is called "heaven." Heaven is the ultimate end and fulfillment of the deepest human longings, the state of supreme, definitive happiness." (n.1024)
>
> Today we will try to understand the biblical meaning of "heaven," in order to have a better understanding of the reality to which this expression refers.
>
> In biblical language "heaven," when it is joined to the "earth," indicates part of the universe. Scripture says about creation: "In the beginning God created the heavens and the earth." (Gn. 1:1)

HEAVEN IS THE TRANSCENDENT DWELLING-PLACE OF THE LIVING GOD

Metaphorically speaking, heaven is understood as the dwelling-place of God, who is thus distinguished from human beings (cf. Ps 104:2f; 115:16; Is 66:1). He sees and judges from the heights of heaven (cf. Ps 113:4-9) and comes down when he is called upon (cf. Ps 18:9, 10: 144:5). However the biblical metaphor makes it clear that God does not identify himself with heaven, nor can he be contained in it (cf. 1 Kings 8:27); and this is true, even though in some passages of the First Book of the Maccabees "Heaven" is simply one of God's names (1 Mac 3:18, 19, 50, 60; 4:24, 55).

The depiction of heaven as the transcendent dwelling-place of the living God is joined with that of the place to which believers, through grace, can also ascend, as we see in the Old Testament accounts of Enoch (cf. Gn 5:24) and Elijah (cf. 2 Kings 2:11). Thus heaven becomes an image of life in God. In this sense Jesus spoke of a "reward in heaven" (Mt 5:12) and urges people to "lay up for yourselves treasures in heaven" (ibid., 6:20; cf. 19:21).

The New Testament amplifies the idea of heaven in relation to the mystery of Christ. To show that the Redeemer's sacrifice acquires perfect and definitive value, the Letter to the Hebrews says that Jesus "passed through the heavens" (Heb 4:14), and entered, not into a sanctuary made with hands, a copy of the true one, but into heaven itself" (ibid., 9:24). Since believers are loved in a special way by the Father, they are raised with Christ and made citizens of heaven. It is worthwhile listening to what the Apostle Paul tells us about this in a very powerful text: "God, who is rich in mercy, out of the great love with which he loved us, even when we were dead through our trespasses, made us alive together with Christ (by grace you have been saved), and raised us up with him, and made us sit with him in the heavenly places in Christ Jesus, that in the coming ages he might show the immeasurable riches of his grace in kindness toward us in Christ Jesus" (Eph 2:4-7). The fatherhood of God, who is rich in mercy, is experienced by creatures through the love of God's crucified and risen Son, who sits in heaven on the right hand of the Father as Lord.

After the course of our earthly life, participation in complete intimacy with the Father thus comes through our insertion into Christ's paschal mystery. St. Paul emphasizes our meeting with Christ in heaven at the end of time with a vivid spatial image: "Then we who are alive, who are left, shall be caught up together with them in the clouds to meet the Lord in the air; and so we shall always be with the Lord. Therefore comfort one another with these words" (1 Thess 4:17-18).

SACRAMENTAL LIFE IS
ANTICIPATION OF HEAVEN

In the context of Revelation, we know that the "heaven" or "happiness" in which we will find ourselves is neither an abstraction nor a physical place in the clouds, but a living, personal relationship with the Holy Trinity. It is our meeting with the Father which takes place in the risen Christ through the communion of the Holy Spirit.

It is always necessary to maintain a certain restraint in describing these "ultimate realities' since their depiction is always unsatisfactory. Today, personalist language is better suited to describing the state of happiness and peace we will enjoy in our definitive communion with God.

The *Catechism of the Catholic Church* sums up the Church's teaching on this truth: "By his death and Resurrection, Jesus Christ has 'opened' heaven to us. The life of the blessed consists in the full and perfect possession of the fruits of the redemption accomplished by Christ. He makes partners in his heavenly glorification those who have believed in him and remained faithful to his will. Heaven is the blessed community of all who are perfectly incorporated into Christ" (n. 1026).

This final state, however, can be anticipated in some way today in sacramental life, the center of which is the Eucharist, and in the gift of self through fraternal charity. If we are able to enjoy properly the good things that the Lord showers upon us every day, we will already have begun to experience that joy and peace which one day will be completely ours. We know that on this earth everything is subject to limits, but the thought of the "ultimate" realities helps us to live better the "penultimate" realities. We know that as we pass through this world we are called to seek "the things that are above, where Christ is seated at the right hand of God" (Col 3:1), in order to be with him in the eschatological fulfillment, when the Spirit will fully reconcile with the Father "all things, whether on earth or in heaven" (Col 1:20).

PART II

INSIDE HELL

CHAPTER NINE

THE NEED FOR JUSTICE

T he earliest accounts of Hell, like those of Heaven, are found in
ancient Persia, where four thousand years ago the
Mesopotamians began to scratch out on baked, clay tablets the
story of a frightful netherworld of the dead—one reserved for the
damned.

Belief in an eternal life of the soul served as the foundation for
these primitive accounts of Hell. But ancient Sumerians, Akkadians,
Babylonians, Assyrians, and other inhabitants of Mesopotamia also
addressed the notion that not all spirits of the dead deserved to inherit
a blessed afterlife. Eventually through a progressive mythology, or
evolving religious doctrine, the afterlife realm was separated into
kingdoms. These kingdoms were determined by divine justice—
something every soul was thought to confront at the time of death.

In its earliest form, Hell, like Heaven, had certain defining
characteristics. While the abode of the good was conceptualized as
having infinite light and love, the abode of the wicked was thought to
be dark, grim, and bleak. This was the region of the damned, a place
where hatred and anger ruled. Like Heaven, Hell was envisioned as a
place suitable for its deserving inhabitants.

The early Egyptians, like the Mesopotamians, were
introspective enough in their belief system to chart out subterranean
afterlife regions that had sinister, horrid spots that were filled with
troubles and hidden from the gods—a stark contrast to their concept of
paradise.

However, in the teachings of the Persian prophet Zoroaster we
find the earliest similarities to what Christian theology would later come

to define as Hell. Zoroaster taught that two spiritual forces, one good and one evil, were pitted against each other and that this conflict is the true basis for the history of the world. The good or divine force, Ahura Mazda ("Wise Lord") lived above with his angels, while Angra Mainayou ("Evil Spirit") dwelled, along with his devils, in the darkness of Hell—a place beneath the earth. And these underworld beings, tormentors of the world, sought the souls of all living men.

A personal judgement at the end of earthly life was thought to take place for all human beings, and if one's verdict was negative, such a condemnation carried with it a sentence of eternal exile in Hell. While some believe Zoroaster's teachings can be traced to the earlier Vedic faith, it is believed that his writings were the first to develop a complete concept of Hell. Indeed, Zoroaster's Hell was a world of darkness, filth, and death. Souls, at their judgement, literally "fell into Hell" if found to be deserving—a description not much different from what the Virgin Mary reportedly stated in some of her revelations of Hell.

The Greeks and their land of the dead, Hades, a place "below the earth," also contributed to the defining characteristics of Hell. Hades, in some translations, is understood to mean "Hell" or "grave." Ruled by Pluto and Persephone, souls reached it only after being ferried, with a coin in their mouth, across the river Styx. Souls experienced abandonment and isolation and were tormented by monsters and demons. Evil spirits of death roamed the dark abode, and in some versions of Hades, these spirits terrified souls that were journeying to other regions. In Hades an infernal lower region known as Tartarus served as a lower abyss of misery where Zeus hurled rebel gods to eternal exile.

By the 5th century BC, judges of an underworld court were introduced into the mythology, as a clear separation between the abodes of the good and those of the evil were established. In Hades, souls who did evil deeds were believed to be sent to the lower regions where they experienced pain and suffering. Greek philosophers eventually developed a Hell where evil men endured unimaginable and never-ending toil

Around this time, an artist's rendering of the Greek underworld would subsequently influence the history of Hell for centuries. In this mural, a demon is featured that devours flesh, something that became an accepted element of many later conceptions of Hell.

With contributions from the great Greek philosophers Hades eventually became place of "eternal" punishment. Socrates took exception to the notion of "eternal" punishment, but allowed for the possibility that there might be "some" truth in this concept. And that the souls dispatched to such a fate tended to be "public figures," men not known for their virtue. And in Plato's *Republic*, the classic story of Er is told. Er has a vision in which he sees the righteous and sinners being separated at death, ascending and descending to their deserved abodes.

The Romans, borrowing heavily from the Greeks, also came to embrace the underworld anthology. Roman philosophers, like their Greek predecessors, advanced their own stories of life after death. Virgil, like Plato, became recognized for his contributions, especially for a new region of the netherworld, Limbo. But it was the lower world that he vividly depicted, one which contained a prison-like atmosphere, complete with chains, the lash, and unceasing moaning. Hell is under Italy in Virgil's, *Aeneid*, and is filled with howling dogs, dark caves, putrid smells, frightening shrieks, and other terrifying features. Plutarch, another Roman philosopher, also produced a horrifying account of Hell, one filled with the souls of the damned, who were destined to live in fiery seas of boiling liquids and other chambers of physical torment.

But as with Heaven, it is again with the Jews that a defined theological understanding of Hell emerges. While some scholars translate the Hebrew word *Sheol*, which occurs 65 times in the Old Testament, as "Hell," debate still exists over whether or not the Jews viewed Sheol as a place of "eternal" punishment and suffering.

For the early Jews, a person went to *Sheol* after death, which meant the "grave," or "pit." Sheol most often is compared to a prison and is used often in the Old Testament with diverse, inferential meanings. Believed by many writers to have been understood by the ancient Jews as a "dark region in the lower world," Sheol was thought to be the abode of souls, both good and evil. There they existed as ghosts, or shades, and were, according to some interpreters, in a state of chronic thirst. However, after the destruction of the First Temple in 586 BC and the exile of the Jews into Babylon, a more profound concept of Sheol begins to appear, one more similar to today's Christian concept of Hell.

This emerging doctrine, many Christian writers believe,

eventually developed into a clearer conception of Sheol as a place of eternal damnation. By the first century, Fr. Lagrange explains, this revised definition of Sheol had been accepted by the Jews:

> In a learned article on Hell, Mr. M. Richard, has made a deep study of those texts of the Old Testament which prove the existence of hell in the strict sense. Before the time of the prophets, he notes, the condition of the wicked after death remained very obscure although ultramundane sanctions are often affirmed. For example, by Ecclesiastes: "Fear God and keep His commandments....For all these God will bring thee into judgment.
>
> To the great prophets God began to show clear perspectives of the future life. We have already cited some of these texts when speaking of the Last Judgment. Isaias lays open a great prophetic vision of the world beyond. It is the restoration of Israel for all eternity, with new heavens and a new earth: "All flesh shall come to adore before My face, saith the Lord, and they shall go out and see the carcasses of the men that have transgressed against Me. Their worm shall not die and their fire shall not be quenched, and they shall be a loathsome sight to all flesh." All commentators see in this text an affirmation of the last judgment, and under a symbolic form, that of eternal hell. This last text is cited in St. Mark by Jesus Himself, and in St. Luke by St. John the Baptist.
>
> Daniel says more clearly: "Many of those that sleep in the dust of the earth shall awake, some unto life everlasting, and others unto reproach, to see it always." Thus the Old Testament, for the first time, declares the resurrection of sinners to meet a judgment of condemnation.
>
> The Book of Wisdom, after describing the sufferings reserved to the wicked after death, continues: "The just shall live for evermore." It adds: "For to him that is little mercy is granted, but the mighty shall be

mightily tormented." It says of the wicked one: "He returneth to the same out of which he was taken, when his life which was lent him shall be called for again."

Ecclesiasticus speaks in the same sense: "Humble thy spirit very much, for the vengeance of the flesh of the ungodly is fire and worms." In the Second Book of Maccabees we read that the seven brothers, martyrs, were sustained in their suffering by the thought of eternal life. They say to their judge: "The King of the world will raise us up...in the resurrection of eternal life...but thou by the judgment of God shalt receive just punishment for thy pride."

All these texts of the Old Testament speak of hell in the proper sense. Many of them affirm the inequality of punishments proportioned to the gravity of the faults committed and unrepented.

Theologians note that numerous Old Testament texts can be understood to be speaking of Hell, in the strictest sense of the word. Isaiah 14:9-15 is often specifically cited:

Hell below was in an uproar to meet thee at thy coming, it stirred up the giants for thee. All the princes of the earth are risen up from their thrones, all the princes of nations. All shall answer, and say to thee, Thou also art wounded as well as we, thou art become like unto us. Thy pride is brought down to hell, thy carcass is fallen down: under thee shall the moth be strewed, and worms shall be thy covering. How art thou fallen from heaven, O Lucifer, who didst rise in the morning; how art thou fallen to the earth, that didst wound the nations? And thou saidst in thy heart: I will ascend into heaven. I will exalt my throne above the stars of God, I will sit in the mountain of the covenant, in the sides of the north. I will ascend above the height of the clouds, I will be like the most High. But yet thou shalt be brought down to hell, into the depth of the pit.

According to St. Alphonsus Liguori, the Old Testament tells us much about Hell and what the Jews came to understand from the teachings of the prophets. Most noted is the reality that Hell is a definite place:

> The Catholic Church teaches that God has established a definite place for the demons and the reprobate as is evident from several texts of Sacred Scripture. St. Jerome deduces this specifically from a passage in the book of Numbers (Num. 16:31-33). Here is described the fate of Dathan and Abiron who were precipitated into Hell, fallen into a chasm which opened under their very feet. At the same time a great flame burst from the earth and killed two hundred and fifty men who were accomplices in their sin. Moreover, in many passages of Sacred Scripture, the word "descent" is used in reference to Hell, indicating that Hell is situated in the bowels of the earth. In another place it is called a "lake"; "Thou hast saved me from those descending into the lake" (Ps. 29:3).

St. Alphonsus Liguori also points out that the Old Testament clearly speaks of the pains of Hell, especially the reality of cold and fire:

> There are numerous texts in Sacred Scripture, however, which demonstrate that the fire of Hell is a true, material and corporeal fire. We read, for instance, in the book of Deuteronomy: "A fire is kindled in my wrath, and shall burn even to the lowest hell" (Deut. 32:22). And in the book of Job: "A fire that is not kindled shall devour him" (Job. 20:26), revealing that his fire of Hell needs not to be nourished, but, once enkindled by God, burns eternally. There are a number of passages in the book of Isaias referring to this fire of Hell: "Which of you can dwell with devouring fire? Which of you shall dwell with everlasting burnings? (33:14); "Their worm shall not die, and their fire shall not be quenched, and they shall be a loathsome sight to

all flesh" (66:24). "He will give fire, and worms into their flesh, that they may burn, and may feel forever" (Judith 16:21). ... "The vengeance on the flesh of the ungodly is fire and worms" (Eccles 7:19). ... "Let him pass from the snow waters to excessive heat, and his sin even to hell" (Job 24:19).

St. Robert Bellarmine concurred with such teachings, contending that the Old Testament did, in fact, clearly define the pains of Hell:

Job says, they shall be bound over from excess of heat to showers of snow, and from showers of snow to excess of heat. Nor are these things figments of fables of poets. Hear what the Lord says to Job: "Hast thou entered into the storehouses of the snow, or hast thou beheld the treasures of the hail, Which I have prepared for the time of the enemy, against the day of battle and war?" (Job 38:28,23). Hear the Psalmist: "Fire and brimstone and storms of winds shall be the portion of their cup" (Ps. 10:7). And if this "portion" is so bitter, what shall it be to drink the whole of the chalice? This great wheel shall turn without end. The Psalmist says: "They are laid in hell like sheep: death shall feed upon them" (Ps. 48:15).

St. Alphonsus also noted how the Old Testament addressed the pains of conscience that souls in Hell are believed to have, as well as their sufferings from devils and darkness:

In addition to their sufferings from the heat and cold of the fire of Hell, Sacred Scripture enumerates a number of other torments which will afflict the damned. One of these is the "worm," to which the Scripture refer frequently. Some commentators have explained this "worm" as a material thing, which will feed upon, without consuming, the flesh of the damned. But most theologians explain it metaphorically as the remorse of conscience which will afflict the damned in the fire and darkness of Hell. Forever will they have imprinted on their memories the results of their sins; forever will they repeat the words ascribed to them in the book of Wisdom: "We have erred from the way of truth, we wearied ourselves in the way of iniquity and destruction and have walked through hard ways. What hath pride profited us? Or what advantage hath the boasting of riches brought us? ... Such things as the sinners said in hell." (Wis. 5:6-14).

Added to their own remorse of conscience, the damned will also be tormented by the reproaches of the demons. This will be one of the most cruel punishments of the damned: the devils, who are their enemies will continually mock them and remind them of their sins. Nor will the suffering of the bodies of the damned cease here. They will also be afflicted by the terrible darkness of Hell, described by the holy man Job: "Before I go, and return no more, to a land that is dark and covered with the mist of death: a land of misery and darkness, where the shadow of death, and no order, but everlasting horror dwelleth" (Job 10:22).

By the 1st century BC, the word *Gehenna*, metaphorically understood as "Hell" and referring to the Gehinnom valley south of Jerusalem, had been included in the Jewish vocabulary . Earlier, fiery pagan child-sacrifices to the God Moloch had taken place in this valley. Later, it was the site of a garbage heap and crematorium. By the time Christ began to firmly establish the existence of Hell by speaking of the fires of Gehenna, theologians say the Jews had no difficulty understanding what He was referring to and, therefore, the seriousness of His Gospel.

CHAPTER TEN

THE FIRES OF GEHENNA

hrist's teachings about Hell were not ambiguous. Rejection of salvation—the salvation Christ said He came to give the world through His own life, death, and resurrection—carried with it a clear and defined consequence. Souls who failed to repent and to choose God were choosing Hell. And once there, opportunities for a soul to repent, Jesus asserted, were forever forfeited.

Tradition maintains that Christ's words, though figurative at times, reveal that Hell was a permanent separation from God, who Christ taught is the source of all life and goodness. As the greatest reward and joy of Heaven was an eternity with God, the gravest punishment and suffering of Hell was, therefore, an eternity apart from God.

But according to theologians, Christ's teachings on Hell also indicate that Hell was also a "place" of the damned, one where spiritual anguish and physical sufferings are eternally experienced as the consequence of sin and rejection of God. Theologians say this teaching is uncontestable in the context of Scripture's assurance of a coming resurrection and restoration of the body at the General Judgment. Christ not only invited his followers and listeners to seek the Kingdom above, but He also unceasingly reminded them of the potential danger of ending up in the kingdom below.

The New Testament begins to reveal the reality of Hell even before Christ's active ministry begins. In the Gospel according to Luke, St. John the Baptist clearly makes reference to this reality: "Every tree that is not fruitful will be cut down and thrown into the fire" (Lk 3:9). Later in this same Gospel, John similarly describes the consequences of God's judgment : "His (God's) winnowing fan is in his hand to clear his threshing floor and gather the wheat into his barn, but the chaff he will burn in unquenchable fire" (Lk 3:17).

But Christ's words are stronger still. Jesus speaks of "everlasting" sin (Mk 3:29, Mt 12:32, and Jn 8:20-29,35) and warns how weakness of the flesh leads to an afterlife of "everlasting torment of that same flesh," if one is not careful: "What I say to you is; everyone who grows angry with his brothers shall be liable to judgment; any man who uses abusive language toward his brother shall be answerable to the Sanhedrin, and if he holds him in contempt he risks the fires of Gehenna," for it is "better to love part of your body than to have it all cast into Gehenna. ... Again, if your right hand is your trouble, cut it off and throw it away! Better to lose part of your body than to have it all cast into Gehenna" (Mt 5:22,29,30). This teaching is found in the parables of the royal marriage, the talents, and the wise and foolish virgins.

Moreover, regardless of the type of sin, Christ teaches that failure to turn to God for forgiveness is equally damning. For a lack of faith in God's mercy is said to be as serious and dangerous as sinning, if not more. At Capernaum, after praising the faith of the centurion and announcing the coming conversion of the Gentiles, Jesus admonishes the Jews for their dangerous lack of faith: "I assure you, I have never found this much faith in Israel. Mark, what I say! Many will come from the east and the west and will find a place at the banquet in the Kingdom of God with Abraham, Isaac, and Jacob, while the natural heirs of the Kingdom will be driven out into the dark. Wailing will be heard there, and grinding of teeth" (Mt 7:10-12).

Scholars note how Jesus referred to sounds emanating from Hell to confirm that it was, in fact, a "place." The phrase "grinding of teeth" occurs six times in the Gospel according to Matthew and is used again in Christ's teaching in Luke on the "narrow door":

> He went through cities and towns teaching—all the while making his way toward Jerusalem. Someone asked him, "Lord, are they few in number who are to be saved?" He replied: "Try to come in through the narrow door. Many, I tell you, will try to enter and be unable. When once the master of the house has risen to lock the door and you stand outside knocking and saying, 'Sir open for us,' he will say in reply, 'I do not know where

you come from.' Then you will begin to say, 'We ate and drank in your company. You taught in our streets.' But he will answer, 'I tell you, I do not know where you come from. Away from me, you evildoers!'

There will be wailing and grinding of teeth when you see Abraham, Isaac, Jacob, and all the prophets safe in the kingdom of God, and you yourselves rejected. People will come from the east and the west, from the north and the south, and will take their place at the feast in the kingdom of God. Some who are last will be first and some who are first will be last. (Lk 13:22-30).

When Jesus addresses the Apostles regarding their fear, he again speaks specifically about the existence of Hell and it's defining characteristics: "Do not fear those who deprive the body of life but cannot destroy the soul. Rather, fear him who can destroy both body and soul in Gehenna" (Mt 10:28). Likewise, in His condemnation of the Pharisees, Christ warns of Hell, saying, "Vipers! Brood of serpents! How can you escape condemnation to Gehenna?" (Mt 23:33). And again, in the Gospel according to John, Jesus explains that "a man who does not live in me is like a withered rejected branch, picked up to be thrown in the fire and burnt" (Jn 15:6).

However, it is especially in Christ's discourse on the final judgement at the end of the world that we find His most graphic description of Hell and its everlasting properties:

> Then the just will ask him: "Lord, when did we see you hungry and feed you or see you thirsty and give you drink? When did we welcome you away from home or clothe you in your nakedness? When did we visit you when you were ill or in prison?" The king will answer them: "I assure you, as often as you did it for one on my least brothers, you did it for me."
>
> Then he will say to those on his left "Out of my sight you condemned, into that everlasting fire prepared for the devil and his angels. I was hungry and you gave me no food, I was thirsty and you gave me no drink. I was away from home and you gave me no welcome, naked

and you gave me no clothing. I was ill and in prison and you did not come to comfort me." Then they in turn will ask: "Lord, when did we see you hungry or thirsty or away from home or naked or ill or in prison and not attend you in your needs?" He will answer them: "I assure you, as often as you neglected to do it to one of these least ones, you neglected to do it to me. These will go to eternal punishment and the just to eternal life." (Mt 25:37-46)

Theologians cite an equally compelling Scripture passage on the reality of Hell—Christ's parable of the rich man and Lazarus, the beggar:

And it came to pass that the beggar died, and was carried by the angels into Abraham's bosom. And the rich man also died; and he was buried in hell. And lifting up his eyes, when he was in torments, he saw Abraham afar off, and Lazarus in his bosom: And he cried, and said: "Father Abraham, have mercy on me, and send Lazarus, that he may dip the tip of his finger in water to cool my tongue: for I am tormented in this flame." And Abraham said to him: "Son, remember that thou didst receive good things in thy lifetime, and likewise Lazarus, evil things, but now is comforted; and thou art tormented. And besides all this, between us and you, there is fixed great chaos; so that they who would pass from hence to you, cannot, nor from thence, come hither." (Lk 16: 22-29)

In support of previous Scripture, the Epistles do not contradict, modify, or back away from Christ's doctrine of Hell. St. Paul writes powerfully about eternal death and of those who will perish and not enter the kingdom (Gal 5:19-21; Eph 5:5; I Cor 6:9-10). They are, Paul says, "on their way to destruction" (2 Cor 2:15, 4:3, 13:5). What is this destruction? The condemnation of Hell! Paul compares it in 1 Timothy 3:6 to "the punishment once meted out to the devil." Likewise, St. Peter speaks of eternal loss (2 Pet 2:1-4, 12, 14, 3:7) and St. James of judgment without mercy (James 2:13).

Fr. Lagrange suggests that full effect of this teaching is most evident in *The Book of Revelation*:

Lastly, the *Apocalypse* contrasts the victory of Christ in the heavenly Jerusalem with the damnation of all those who will be thrown into the abyss of fire and sulphur. This eternal damnation is called second death. It is the privation of divine life, of the vision of God, in a place of eternal punishment, where those will be tormented by fire who wear the sign of the beast, and hence are excluded from the book of life.

This is the doctrine already announced by the great prophets and in particular by Isaias. From the time of these prophets to the Apocalypse the revelation about eternal hell-fire never ceased to become more precise, just as the doctrine of eternal life became more precise. Among these punishments we find those of loss, of fire, of inequality in pain, of eternal duration. Mortal sin unrepented has left the soul in a habitual state of rebellion against an infinite good.

From a purely doctrinal standpoint, the Gospels and the Epistles establish that, according to Christ, Hell exists as a "condition" and a "place." Based on Scripture, we know that Hell is dark, horrific, and unending. It is a place where souls suffer not only pain of the senses but spiritual torment because of separation from God.

Each of the following teachings is supported by Holy Scripture:

HELL IS A PLACE OF SUFFERING

- Then shall he say to them also that shall be on his left hand: Depart from me, you cursed, into everlasting fire, which was prepared for the devil and his angels.... And thee shall go into everlasting punishment (Mt 25: 41–46).

- And the third angel followed them, saying with a loud voice: If any man shall adore the beast and his image, and receive his character in his forehead, or in his hand; He also shall drink of the wine of the wrath of God, which is mingled with pure wine in the cup of his wrath, and shall be tormented with fire and brimstone in the sight of the holy angels, and in the sight of the Lamb. And the smoke of their torments shall ascend up for ever and ever: neither have they rest day nor night, who have adored the beast and his image, and whoever receiveth the character of his name (Rv 14:20).

- And the beast was taken, and with him the false prophet, who wrought signs before him, wherewith he seduced them who received the character of the beast, and who adored his image. These two were cast alive into the pool of fire, burning with brimstone (Rv 20:9-10).

- And there came down fire from God out of heaven, and devoured them; and the devil, who seduced them, was cast into the pool of fire and brimstone, where both the beast and the false prophet shall be tormented day and night for ever and ever (Rv 20: 9-10).

- But the fearful, and unbelieving, and the abominable, and murderers, and whoremongers, and sorcerers, and idolaters, and all liars, they shall have their portion in the pool burning with fire and brimstone, which is the second death (Rv 21:8).

HELL IS ETERNAL

- I indeed baptize you in water unto penance, but he that shall come after me, is mightier than I, whose shoes I am not worthy to bear; he shall baptize you in the Holy Ghost and fire. Whose fan is in his hand, and he will thoroughly cleanse his floor, and gather his wheat into the barn; but the chaff he will burn with unquenchable fire (Mt 3: 11-12).

- Then he shall say to them also that shall be on his left hand: Depart from me, you cursed, into everlasting fire which was prepared for the devil and his angels.... And these shall go into everlasting punishment: but the just, into life everlasting (Mt 25: 41-46).

- And if thy hand scandalize thee, cut it off: it is better for thee to enter life, maimed, then having two hands to go into hell, into unquenchable fire: Where their worm dieth not, and the fire is not extinguished. (Mk 4: 42-43).

- And Abraham said to him (Dives): Son, remember that thou didst receive good things in thy lifetime, and likewise Lazarus evil things, but now he is comforted; and thou art tormented. And besides all this, between us and you, there is fixed a great chaos: so that they who would pass from hence to you, cannot, nor from thence come hither (Lk 16:25-26).

- And to you who are troubled, rest with us when the Lord Jesus shall be revealed from heaven, with the angles of his power: In a flame of fire, giving vengeance to them who know not God, and who obey not the gospel of our Lord Jesus Christ. Who shall suffer eternal punishment in destruction, from the face of the lord, and from the glory of his power (2 These 1:7-9).

- And the angels who kept not their principality, but forsook their own habitation, he hath reserved under darkness in everlasting chains, unto the judgement of the great day. As Sodom and Gomorrah, and the neighboring cities, in like manner, having given themselves to fortification, and going after other flesh, were made an example, suffering the punishment of eternal fire. In like manner these men also defile the flesh, and despite dominion, and blaspheme majesty....Raging waves of the sea, foaming out their own confusion; wandering stars to whom the storm of darkness is reserved for ever (Jude 1. 6-8, 13).

- And the smoke of their torments shall ascend up for ever and ever: neither have they rest day nor night, who have adored the beast, and his image, and whoever receiveth the character of his name (Rv 14:11).

- And there came down fire from God out of heaven, and devoured them; and the devil, who seduced them, was cast into the pool of fire and brimstone, where both the beast, and the false prophets, shall be tormented day and night, for ever and ever (Rv 20:9-10).

- And whosoever shall speak a word against the Son of man, it shall be forgiven him: but he that shall speak against the Holy Ghost, it shall not be forgiven him, neither in this world, not in the world to come (Mt 12:32).

- But he that shall blaspheme against the Holy Ghost, shall never have forgiveness, but shall be guilty of an everlasting sin (Mk 3:29).

- Know you not that the unjust shall not possess the kingdom of God? Do not err: neither fornicators, nor idolaters, nor adulterers, nor the effeminate, nor liars with mankind, nor thieves, nor covetous, nor drunkards, nor railers, nor extortioners, shall possess the kingdom of God (1 Cor 6:9-10).

- Now the works of the flesh are manifest, which are fornication, uncleanness, immodesty, luxury, idolatry, witchcraft, enmities, contentions, emulations, wraiths, quarrels, dissension, sects, envies, murders, drunkenness, revels, and such like. Of the which, I foretell you, as I have foretold to you, that they who do such things shall not obtain the kingdom of God (Gal 3, 19-21).

HELL IS DARK AND HORRENDOUS

- And the unprofitable servant cast ye out into the exterior darkness. There shall be weeping and gnashing of teeth (Mt 25:30).

- And the angels who kept not their principality, but forsook their own habitation, he hath reserved under darkness in everlasting chains, unto the judgement of the great day (Jude 1: 6).

- Raging waves of the sea, foaming out their own confusion; wandering stars, to whom the storm of darkness is reserved for ever (Jude 1:13).

PAIN OF THE SENSES IN HELL

- And fear ye not them that kill the body, and are not able to kill the soul: but rather fear him that can destroy both soul and body in hell (Mt 10:28).

- The son of man shall send his angels, and they shall gather out of his kingdom all scandals, and them that work iniquity. And shall cast them into the furnace of fire: there shall be weeping and gnashing of teeth (Mt 8: 41- 42).

- And if thy hand scandalize thee, cut it off: it is better for thee to enter into life, maimed, than having two hands to go into hell, into unquenchable fire: Where their worm dieth not, and the fire, is not extinguished (Mk 9: 42 - 43).

- Whose fan is in his hand, and he will purge his floor, and will gather the wheat into his barn; but the chaff he will burn with unquenchable fire (Lk 3:17).

- And it came to pass, that the beggar died, and was carried by the angels into Abraham's bosom. And the rich man also died: and he was buried in hell. And lifting up his eyes when he was in torments, he saw Abraham after off and Lazarus in his bosom: And he cried, and said: Father Abraham, have mercy on me, and send Lazarus, that he may dip the tip of his finger in water, to cool my tongue: for I am tormented in this flame. And Abraham said to him: Son, remember that thou didst receive good things in thy lifetime, and likewise Lazarus evil things, but now he is comforted; and thou art tormented (Lk 16:22-25).

- If any one abide not in me, he shall be cast forth as a branch, and shall wither, and they shall gather him up and cast him into the fire, and he burneth (Jn 15:6).

- For we must all be manifested before the judgment seat of Christ, that everyone may receive the proper things of the body, according as he hath done whether it be good or evil (1 Cor 5:10).

- And hell and death were cast into the pool of fire. This is the second death. And whosoever was not found written in the book of life, was cast into the pool of fire (Rv 20:14-15).

- But the fearful, and unbelieving, and the abominable, and murderers, and whoremongers, and sorcerers, and idolaters, and all liars, they shall have their portion in the pool burning with fire and brimstone, which is the second death (Rv 21:8).

Scripture, then, clearly establishes that Hell is a place and a condition of the damned, that it is an abode of pain and darkness, and that once there, no escape is possible. In fact, beyond the Gospel's direct references to Hell, there are also many indirect statements made by Christ which allude to Hell, such as, "It were better for him, if that man had not been born" (Mt 26:24), and, "What doth it profit a man if he gaineth whole world, and suffers the loss of his own soul? Or what exchange shall a man give for his soul?" (Mt 16:25).

Indeed, from Christ's admonition to "judge not, that you may not be judged" (Mt 5: 37) to his warning that "it easier for a camel to pass through the eye of a needle, than for a rich man to enter the Kingdom of God" (Mk 10:25), we see that the "Good News" of the New Testament points always toward salvation and Heaven. However, it is a salvation that cannot occur and a Heaven that cannot be reached without judgement—a judgement that puts each and every soul face to face with the possibility of either eternal life in Heaven or eternal damnation in Hell.

CHAPTER ELEVEN

AN UNQUENCHABLE FIRE

The Fathers of the Church, with few exceptions, were united in teaching the doctrine of an eternal Hell. It is a truth, the Fathers stated, that divine justice is revealed in Scripture and should not be explained away: "It is a fearful thing to fall into the hands of the living God" (Heb 10:31).

The early Church was firm on the doctrine of Hell. It was reasonably certain, the Fathers insisted, and their words substantiate their position. St. Justin wrote in the second century that "if Hell does not exist, either there is no God, or if there is, He does not concern Himself with men, and virtue and vice have no meaning. Instead of complaining about the eternity of the pains of Hell, the sinner ought to make every effort to die a happy death. Persevering prayer will obtain this grace for him. 'Watch ye and pray,' is Our Lord's admonition to all of us, 'because ye know not the day nor the hour.'"

St. John Chysostom also spoke out about the existence of Hell: "You see that not only those who rob and cheat, those who do evil, but that also those who omit to do good are punished with eternal suffering."

Sts. Methodius, Cyril of Jerusalem, Epiphanus, Basil, Ephrem, and Jerome, likewise, upheld the doctrine of Hell. On May 20, 325, the First Ecumenical Council opened at Nicea. Four weeks later the Council agreed on the Creed, a clear and concise statement of the Catholic faith in the divinity of Christ. The Nicene Creed firmly established that a judgment of the living and the dead was to be expected.

In the 6th century, the Council at Constantinople stated, "If anyone says or holds, that the punishment of devils and wicked men is temporary and will eventually cease, that is to say that devils or the ungodly will be completely restored to their original state, let him be anathema."

But though the early Church is almost unanimous on the doctrine of Hell, it was not until the 5th century that St. Augustine defined a precise theology of Hell in his classic work, *City of God*:

> Hell, which is also called a lake of fire and brimstone, will be material fire, and will torment the bodies of the damned, whether men or devils—the solid bodies of the one, and the aerial bodies of the others. Or, if only men have bodies as well as souls, still the evil spirits, even without bodies, will be connected to the fires as to receive pain without bestowing life. One fire certainly shall be the lot of both.

St. Augustine wrote that no one was exempt from divine justice and that clearly God used His capacity to inflict the punishment of Hell eternally. Offering proof from Scripture and the applicable knowledge of his day, Augustine carefully explained why Hell existed, what it consisted of, and why it's reality is undeniable. Indeed, St. Augustine's writings are profound and deserve an extended look:

> It is not easy to find a proof that will convince unbelievers of the possibility of human bodies remaining in merely active, alive, and uncorrupted after death, but also of continuing forever in the torments of fire. Such unbelievers are deaf of forever in the torments of the fire. Such unbelievers are deaf to any appeal to the power of the Almighty, and demand a demonstration in terms of positive facts. When facts are reported, they deny the value of the evidence; when the evidence is produced, they declare it inconclusive. In regard to facts, it is said that certain animals live in fire, although they are mortal and, therefore, corruptible; that in certain hot springs, too hot for a hand to bear, there is found a species of worm that not merely endures the

heat but cannot live without it. But even when the unbelievers see such things with their eyes (or accept reliable witnesses), they object, first, that the animals feel no pain from the heat but, in fact, thrive in it. Strange unbelievers, who find it easier to believe that animals can thrive in fire than survive the pain! Surely, if it is still more incredible that it should live in a fire and not feel it. No one who can believe the second marvel has a right to doubt the first.

One thing that will happen, and most certainly happen, is what God, through His Prophet, said concerning the punishment of hell being eternal: "Their worm shall not die, and their fire shall not be quenched." And it was to emphasize this further that, when the Lord Jesus was counseling us to cut off members that scandalize us (meaning that we should cut off people whom we love as we love our right hand), He said: "It is better for thee to enter into life maimed, than, having two hands, to go into hell, into the unquenchable fire, where their worm dies not, and the fire is not quenched." And for the eye, too: "If is better for thee to enter into the kingdom of God with one eye than, having two eyes, to be cast into hell fire, where their worm dies not, and the fire is not quenched." He did not hesitate and that emphatic warning, coming from divine lips, are enough to make any man tremble.

There are some who think that both the "fire" and the "worm" here mentioned are meant as pains of the soul rather than the body. Their argument is that, since those who repent too late and, therefore, in vain (because cut off from the kingdom of God) burn with anguish of soul, the "fire" can be taken very well to symbolize this burning anguish. They quote the words of the Apostle: "Who is made to stumble, and not be inflamed?" They hold that the "worm" also must be taken to mean the soul, as can be seen, they think, in the text: "As a moth doth by a garment, and a worm by the wood, so the sadness of a man consumeth the heart."

However, those who have no doubt that in hell there will be sufferings for both soul and body hold that the body will be burned in fire while the soul will be gnawed, as it were, by the "worm" of grief. This is certainly a probable enough view, since it is absurd to think that either pain of body or anguish of soul will be lacking there. For myself, however, it seems preferable to say that both "fire" and the "worm" apply to the body, and that the reason for making no mention in Scripture of the anguish of the soul is that it is implied, though not made explicit. When the body is in such pain, the souls must be tortured by fruitless repentance. Take, for example, this test of the Old Testament: "The vengeance on the flesh of the ungodly." What, then, could have been the reason for saying "on the flesh of the ungodly," except that both "fire" and the "worm" are to serve as punishment for the body? However, it may be argued that "vengeance on the flesh" was meant to imply that the vengeance is to fall on man, in so far as he has lived according to the flesh. In support of this interpretation, there are the words of St. Paul: "For if you live according to the flesh you will die, words implying that is because a man lives according to the flesh that he will suffer the "second death." Thus, each of us is free to make his own choice, either attributing "fire" (taken literally) to the body, and the "worm" (in a figurative sense) to the soul, attributing both "fire" and the "worm," in their literal meanings, to the body.

Suffice it to say that argument enough was given above to prove, first, that living creatures can continue in fire without being consumed and in pain without suffering death; second, that this is in virtue of a miracle of the omnipotent Creator; and, third, that anyone who denies the possibility of this miracle is simply unaware of the Source of all that is wonderful in all natures whatsoever. This Source is God. It is He who made all the natural marvels, great and small, which I have mentioned and incomparably more which I did not mention, and it is He who embraced all these miracles within a single universe which is itself the greatest of all these natural miracles. And so, I repeat, each one is free to choose whichever of the two interpretations he finds more satisfactory, namely, that the "worm," too, in its literal sense, applies to the body or the soul. Which of the two views is true the future reality will be in need of no experience of these sufferings but only of that full and perfect wisdom which will suffice to teach them all such truth; for, now we know in "part," waiting for the time "when that which is perfect has come." The one thing which we may by no means believe is that bodies in hell will be such that they will be unaffected by any pains inflicted by fire.

Over the centuries, many great leaders of the Church have concurred with St. Augustine on the reality and pains of Hell:

St. Bonaventure: "The most terrible penalty of the damned is being shut out forever from the blissful and joyous contemplation of the Blessed Trinity."
St. Alphonsus Laager: "If Hell were not eternal, it would not be Hell."
St. Basil: "The Lord will divide the fire from the light, so that this fire will only perform the office of burning, and not of giving light."
St. Thomas Aquinas: "The pain of the damned is infinite, because it is the loss of an infinite good."
St. Bernard: "There (Hell) fire consumes that it may always preserve."
Esubius Emissenus: "There will be a way to descend (into Hell) but none to ascend."
Tertullian: "Hence the dammed not only suffer what they suffer each moment, but they suffer in each moment the pain of eternity saying: "What I now suffer, I shall have to suffer forever."
St. Bernard of Siena: "By every mortal sin an infinite injury is done to God; and to an infinite injury an infinite

punishment is due."

Pope Innocent III: "The reprobate will not humble themselves, but the malignancy of hating will go on in them."

St. Cyril of Alexandria: "The damned cry from the pit of Hell, but no one comes to deliver them from it; and no compassionates for them."

St. Thomas Aquinas: "Suffering is proportioned, not to the duration of sin, but to its gravity. A deed of assassination, which lasts a few minutes, merits death or life imprisonment. A momentary act of betrayal merits permanent exile. But mortal sin has a gravity without measure. Further, it remains as a habitual disorder, in itself irreparable, which merits punishment without end."

St. Robert Bellarmine: "My dear people, compare this punishment of the martyrs with the tortures of the damned. In the dungeon of the confessors of Christ, there were but few people. In the dungeon of Hell their shall be innumerable people. In the former, only the filth of human beings aroused the stench. In the latter, all the filth, dung, foulness and heavy stench of the whole world shall be gathered together. If, then, the stench of that earthly dungeon surpassed all manner of punishments, who shall be able to bear the incomparably heavier and more horrible stench of Hell? Who can read without horror of that novel kind of torment, whether it is true or fictitious, which the Latin poet describes when he says:

> Indeed, he joined dead bodies to living ones, Linking hand to hand and mouth to mouth. Singular torment: He killed them slowly, And, in grim embrace, they flowed with slime and gore."
> (Virgil, *Aeneid*, Book 8, Lines 485–488)

Church Councils have consistently upheld and defined the

doctrine of Hell. After the Council of Trent in the 17th century, the Church issued an authoritative Catechism on its teachings, which included its doctrine on Hell:

THE CATECHISM OF TRENT

Turning next to those who shall stand on His left, He (Christ) will pour out His justice upon them in these words: *Depart from me, ye cursed, into everlasting fire, prepared for the devil and his angels.*

The first words, *depart from me,* express the heaviest punishment with which the wicked shall be visited, their eternal banishment from the sight of God, unrelieved by one consolatory hope of ever recovering so great a good. This punishment is called by theologians *the pain of loss,* because in hell the wicked shall be deprived forever of light of vision of God.

The words *ye cursed,* which follow, increase unutterably their wretched and calamitous condition. If when banished from the divine presence they were deemed worthy to receive some benediction, this would be to them a great source of consolation. But since they can expect nothing of this kind as an alleviation of their misery, the divine justice deservedly pursues them with every species of malediction, once they have been banished.

The next words, *into everlasting fire,* express another sort of punishment, which is called by theologians *the pain of sense,* because, like lashes, stripes or other more severe chastisements , among which fire, no doubt, produces the most intense pain, it is felt through the organs of sense. When, moreover, we reflect that this torment is to be eternal, we can see at once that the punishment of the damned includes every kind of suffering.

The concluding words, *which was prepared for the devil and his angels,* make this still more clear. For since nature has so provided that we feel miseries less when we have companions and shares in them who can, at least in some measure, assist us by their advice and kindness, what must be the horrible state of the damned who in such calamities can never separate themselves justly shall this very sentence be pronounced by our Lord and Saviour on those sinners who neglected all the works of true mercy, who gave neither food to the hungry, nor drink to the thirsty, who refused shelter to the stranger and clothing to the naked, and who would not visit the sick and the imprisoned.

THE CATECHISM OF THE CATHOLIC CHURCH (1994)

We cannot be united with God unless we freely choose to love him. But we cannot love God if we sin gravely against him, against our neighbor or against ourselves: "He who does not love remains in death. Anyone who hates his brother is a murdered, and you know that no murderer has eternal life abiding in him." Our Lord warns us that we shall be separated from him if we fail to meet the serious needs of the poor and the little ones who are his brethren. To die in mortal sin without repenting and accepting God's merciful love means remaining separated from him forever by our own free choice. This state of definitive self-exclusion from communion with God and the blessed is called "hell."

Jesus often speaks of "Gehenna," of "the unquenchable fire" reserved for those who to the end of their lives refuse to believe and be converted, where both soul and body can be lost. Jesus solemnly proclaims that he "will send his angels, and they will gather.. all evil doers, and throw them in to the furnace of fire," and that he will pronounce the condemnation: "Depart from me, you cursed, into the eternal fire!"

The teaching of the Church affirms the existence of hell and its eternity. Immediately after death the souls of those who die in a state of mortal sin descend into hell, where they suffer the punishments of hell, "eternal fire." The chief punishment of hell is eternal separation from

God, in whom alone man can possess the life and happiness for which he was created and for which he longs.

The affirmations of Sacred Scripture and the teachings of the Church on the subject of hell are a *call to the responsibility* incumbent upon man to make use of his freedom in view of his eternal destiny. They are at the same time an urgent *call to conversion*: "Enter by the narrow gate; for the gate is wide and the way is easy that leads to destruction, and those who enter by it are many. For the gate is narrow and the way is hard, that leads to life, and those who find it are few:

> Since we know neither the day nor the hour, we should follow the advice of the Lord and watch constantly so that, when the single course of our earthly life is completed, we may merit to enter with him into the marriage feast and be numbered among the blessed, and not, like the wicked and slothful servants, be ordered to depart into the their eternal fire, into the outer darkness where "men will weep and gnash their teeth."

God predestines no one to go to hell; for this, a willful turning away from God (a mortal sin) is necessary, and persistence in it until the end. In the Eucharistic liturgy and in the daily prayers of her faithful, the Church implores the mercy of God, who does not "want any to perish, but all to come to repentance":

> Father, accept this offering from your whole family. Grant us your peace in this life, save us from final damnation, and count us among those you have chosen.

CHAPTER TWELVE

"I AM IN HERE FOR ALL ETERNITY"

There is no lack of private revelation concerning Hell. Many souls have reportedly been shown Hell, like Heaven and Purgatory, in dreams or visions. These revelations, which often include an angel, the Virgin Mary, or Jesus as a guide can be traced back to the earliest days of the Church.

Many mystics, after their "tour" of Hell, describe it as a "fiery pit" wreaking of horrid smells and quaking with terrible sounds. Beasts, worms, fire, snow, blood, chains, and legions of rebel angels are featured in these alleged accounts.

By the early Middle Ages, theologians wrestled with certain questions regarding Hell. What size is it? What sins merit condemnation? What is the difference between Personal and General Judgement? Where in Hell did Jesus descend after his crucifixion? Where is Limbo? Who was Satan? As the questions emerged so did the revelations.

Although the foundation for the doctrine on Hell was already established, and private revelation added nothing really "new," these mystical dreams and visions did illustratively support the accepted view of Hell as "abominable."

As with the personal accounts of Heaven and Purgatory, this "vision literature" on Hell served as a dramatic teaching tool. Many of the faithful began to invite such experiences, and priests directed those visionaries they considered authentic to write down such revelations.

As he did in assembling accounts of Purgatory in his famous work, *Dialogues* (590 A.D.), Pope St. Gregory the Great collected revelations of Hell. One account was from a monk, "Peter of Spain" who claimed to have seen many rich, powerful, and famous people suspended amidst flames. Another account, by a man named Repartus, involved a dream in which he saw a huge bonfire being prepared for a priest. A similar account involved a dying man who, destined for Hell, repented after receiving news of a prophetic vision in which he was dragged off to a dark place by "disgusting people that had flames spewing from their mouths and noses." The repentant man died a week later. Clearly, St. Gregory's collected writings portrayed Hell in the traditional sense of fire, smoke, filth, repugnant smells, and blackness.

Around the same time, St. Gregory of Tour's (539-594) *History of the Franks* reported a vision of Hell that described fiery rivers crowded with the souls of sinful clergy. Venerable Bede (673-735), an English monk, also chronicled visions of Hell during this period. In his *Ecclesiastical History of England*, Bede wrote of two visions of Hell. According to Alice Turner, in *The History of Hell*, Bede wrote of a vision given to him by a man named Furseus who, in 633, had several visions, including one of Hell.

Escorted in the air by angels, Furseus flies over a dark valley that has four fires containing the souls of four different kinds of sinners. These flames merge into one, and then Furseus witnesses devils floating in the air, tormenting sinners that he had once known. Bede says that Furseus displayed burns on his body that scarred in such a way as to appear to be evidence of his flight into Hell.

Turner recounts another of Bede's recorded visions of Hell which refer to a man named Drythelm. This man was supposedly led by an angel to a valley of fire where he witnessed, at the far end, a pit with human souls falling in and out. Evil spirits, lamentations and dreadful laughter accompanied the trip to the pit. Drythelm himself was almost attacked by the devils were it not for the protective efforts of his angel.

By the 12th century, vision literature continued to grow in popularity. The *Vision of Tundal* (1149), written by an Irish monk, was the most popular account. It was reportedly second only to the Bible. According to Turner, Tundal's depiction of Hell is the most famous in Medieval literature. Well written and filled with terrifying details, Tundal sees murderers being grilled over iron gates, mountains of fire, valleys of hot coals, ice, snow, hailstorms, and the torturous experiences of an army of former villains made up of spies and traitors. As Tundal traverses Hell, he sees great devil beasts with flaming eyes, frenzied lions, mad dogs, and serpents. Numerous chambers of Hell are described and in them are priests, nuns, friends, and relatives.

In addition to these descriptive accounts of Hell, "apparitions of the damned" were also collected. These accounts differed from "visions of Hell" in that they involved apparitions of damned souls who were permitted to appear to their friends or family for the sole purpose of demonstrating that Hell did, indeed, exist and that they were now part of it. Typically, these "apparitions of the damned," which provide us with another perspective on the "reality" of Hell, took place almost immediately after the death of the damned soul.

Fr. F. X. Shouppe, who authored a similar 19th century text on Purgatory, recorded many such stories in his book, *Hell.* The following accounts from Fr. Shouppe's book depict these "apparitions of the damned":

> St. Antoniunus (1389-14569), Archbishop of Florence, relates in his writings a terrible fact which, about the middle of the 15th century, spread fright over the whole North of Italy. A young man of good stock, who, at the age of 16 or 17, had had the misfortune of concealing a mortal sin in Confession, and, in that state, of receiving Communion, had put off from week to week and month to month, the painful disclosures of his sacrileges. Tortured by remorse, instead of discovering with simplicity his misfortune, he sought to gain quiet by great penances, but to no purpose. Unable to bear the strain any longer, he entered a monastery; there, at least, he said to himself, I will tell all, and expiate my frightful sins. Unhappily, he was welcomed as a holy young man by his superiors, who knew him by reputation, and his shame again got the better of him. According to the story, he deferred his confession of this sin to a later period; and a year, two years, three years passed in this deplorable state; he never dared to reveal his misfortune. Finally, sickness seemed to him to afford an easy means of doing it. "Now is the time," he said to himself; "I am going to tell all; I will make a general confession before I die." But this time, instead of frankly and fairly declaring his faults, he twisted them so artfully that his confessor was unable to

understand him. He hoped the confessor would come back again the next day, but an attack of delirium came on, and the unfortunate man died.

The community, who were ignorant of the frightful reality, were full of veneration for the deceased. His body was borne with a certain degree of solemnity into the church of the monastery, and lay exposed in the choir until the next morning when the funeral was to be celebrated.

A few hours before the time fixed for the ceremony, one of the Brothers, sent to toll the bell, saw before him, all of a sudden, the deceased, encompassed by chains that seemed aglow with fire, while something blazing appeared all over his person. Frightened, the poor Brother fell on his knees, with his eyes riveted on the terrifying apparition. Then the damned soul said to him: *"Do not pray for me, I am in here for all eternity."* And he related the sad story of his false shame and sacrileges. There upon, he vanished, leaving in the church a disgusting odor, which spread all over the monastery, as if to prove the truth of all the Brother just saw and heard. Notified at once, the Superiors had the corpse taken away, deeming it unworthy of ecclesiastical burial.

★

...It was in Russia, at Moscow, a short while before the horrible campaign of 1812. My maternal grandfather, Count Rostopchine, the Military Governor of Moscow, was very intimate with General Count Orloff, celebrated for his bravery, but as godless as he was brave.

One day, at the close of a supper, Count Orloff and one of his friends, General V., also a disciple of Voltaire, had set to horribly ridiculing religion, especially Hell. *"Yet,"* said Orloff, *"if by chance there should be anything the other side of the curtain?"* *"Well,"* took up General V., *"whichever of us shall depart first will come to inform the other of it. Is it agreed?"*

"An excellent idea," replied Count Orloff, and both interchanged very seriously their word of honor not to miss the engagement.

A few weeks later, one of those great wars which Napoleon had the gift of creating, burst forth. The Russian army began the campaign, and General V. received orders to start out forthwith to take an important command.

He had left Moscow about two or three weeks, when one morning, at a very early hour, while my grandfather was dressing, his chamber door was rudely pushed open. It was Count Orloff, in dressing gown and slippers, his hair on end, his eyes wild, and pale like a dead man. *"What? Orloff, you? At this hour? And in such a costume? What ails you? What has happened?"* *"My dear,"* replied Count Orloff, *"I believe I am beside myself. I have just seen General V. Has General V., then, come back?"* *'Well, no,"* rejoined Orloff, throwing himself on a soda, and holding his head between his hands; *"No, he has not come back, and that is what frightens me!"*

My grandfather did not understand him. He tried to sooth him. *"Relate to me,"* he said to Orloff, *"what happened to you, and what all this means."* Then, striving to stifle his emotion, the Count related the following: *"My dear Rostopchine, some time ago, V. And I mutually swore that the first of us who died should come and tell the other if there is anything on the other side of the curtain. Now this morning, scarcely half an hour since, I was calmly lying awake in my bed, not thinking at all of my friend, when all of a sudden, the curtains of my bed were rudely parted, and at two steps from me I saw General V. Standing up, pal, with his right had on his breast, and saying to me: 'What do we do now? There is a Hell, and I am there! What do we do now?' And he disappeared. I came at once to you. My head is splitting! What a strange thing! I do not know what to think of it.'"*

My grandfather calmed him as well as he could. It was no easy matter. He spoke of hallucinations, nightmares; perhaps he was asleep....There are many

extraordinary unaccountable things.   And other
commonplaces, which constitute the comfort of
freethinkers.   Then he ordered his carriage, and took
Count Orloff back to his hotel.

Now, ten or twelve days after this strange
incident, an army messenger brought my grandfather,
among other news, that of the death of General V.   The
very morning of the day Count Orloff had seen and heard
him, the same hour he appeared at Moscow, the
unfortunate General, reconnoitering the enemy's
position, had been shot through the breast by a bullet and
had fallen stark dead.

★

Mgr. De Segur relates a... fact, which he regards as
free from doubt.   He had learned it in 1859, of a most
honorable priest and superior of an important community.
This priest had the particulars of it from a near relation of
the lady to whom it had happened.   At that time,
Christmas Day, 1859, this person was still living and little
over forty years.

She chanced to be in London in the winter of
1847-1848.   She was a widow, about twenty-nine years
old, quite rich and worldly.   Among the gallants who
frequented her *salon*, there was noticed a young lord,
whose attentions compromised her extremely and whose
conduct, besides, was anything but edifying!

One evening, or rather one night, for it was close
upon midnight, she was reading in her bed some novel,
coaxing sleep. One o'clock struck by the clock; she blew
out her taper.   She was about to fall asleep when, to her
great astonishment, she noticed that a strange, wan
glimmer of light, which seemed to come from the door of
the drawing-room, spread by degrees into her chamber,
and increased momentarily.   Stupefied at first and not
knowing what this meant, she began to get alarmed, when
she saw the drawing-room door slowly open and the

young lord, the partner of her disorders, enter the room. Before she had time to say a single word, he seized her by the left wrist, and with a hissing voice, syllabled to her in English: *"There is a Hell!"* The pain she felt in her arm was so great that she lost her senses.

When, half an hour after, she came to again, she rang for her chambermaid. The latter, on entering, noticed a keen smell of burning. Approaching her mistress, who could hardly speak, she noticed on her wrist so deep a burn that the bone was laid bare and the flesh almost consumed; this burn was the size of a man's hand.

Moreover, she remarked that, from the door of the salon to the bed, and from the bed to that same door, the carpet bore the imprint of a man's steps, which had burned through the stuff. By the directions of her mistress, she opened the drawing-room door; there, more traces were seen on the carpet outside.

The following day, the unhappy lady learned, with a terror easy to be divined, that on that very night, about one o'clock in the morning, her lord had been found dead-drunk under the table, that his servants had carried him to his room, and that there he had died in their arms.

I do not know, added the Superior, whether that terrible lesson converted the unfortunate lady, but what I do not know is that she is still alive and that, to conceal from sight the traces of her ominous burn, she wears on the left wrist, like a bracelet, a wide gold band, which she does not take off day or night. I repeat it, I have all these details from her near relation, a serious Christian, in whose word I repose the fullest belief. They are never spoken of, even in the family; and I confide them to you, suppressing every proper name.

Notwithstanding the disguise beneath which this apparition has been, and must be enveloped, it seems to me impossible, adds Mgr. de Segur, to call into doubt the dreadful authenticity of the details.

★

In the year 1873 a few days before the Assumption, there was an apparition from beyond the grave, which efficaciously confirms the reality of Hell. It was in Rome. A brothel, opened in that city after the Piedmontese invasion, stood near a police station. One of the bad girls who lived there had been wounded in the hand, and it was found necessary to take her to the Hospital of Consolation. Whether her blood, vitiated by bad living, had brought on mortification of the wound, or from an unexpected complication, she nonetheless died suddenly during the night. At the same instant, one of her companions, who surely was ignorant of what had happened at the hospital, began to utter shrieks of despair to the point of awakening the inhabitants of the locality, creating a flurry among the wretched creatures of the house, and provoking the intervention of the police. The dead girl at the hospital, surrounded by flames, had appeared to her and said: *'I am damned! And if you do not wish to be like me, leave this place of infamy and return to God.'*

Nothing could quell the despair of this girl, who, at daybreak, departed, leaving the whole house plunged in a stupor, especially as soon as the death of her companion at the hospital was known.

Just at this period, the mistress of the place, an exalted Garibaldian, and known as such by her brethren and friends, fell sick. She soon sent for a priest to receive the Sacraments. The ecclesiastical authority deputed for this task a worthy prelate, Mgr. Sirolli, the pastor of the parish of Saint-Saviour in Laura. He, fortified by special instructions, presented himself and exacted of the sick woman, before all, in presence of many witnesses, the full and entire retraction of her blasphemies against the Sovereign Pontiff and the discontinuance of the infamous trade she plied. The unhappy creature did so without hesitating, consented to purge her house, then made her confession and received the Holy Viaticum with great sentiments of repentance and humility.

Feeling that she was dying, she besought the good pastor with tears not to leave her, frightened as she always was by the apparition of that damned girl. Mgr. Sirolli, unable to satisfy her on account of the proprieties which would not permit him to spend the night in such a place, sent to the police for two men, closed up the house and remained until the dying woman had breathed her last.

Pretty soon, all Rome became acquainted with the details of these tragic occurrences. As ever, the ungodly and lewd ridiculed them, taking good care not to seek for any information about them; the good profited by them, to become still better and more faithful to their duties.

Though unverifiable, we should respect such "apparitions of the damned" if for no other reason than they demonstrate God's mercy and the many ways He chooses to express it. Perhaps no account is more worthy of mention than that of St. Teresa of Avila, who declared that God had shown her the place that had been reserved for her in Hell.

St. Teresa recalled that one day she was in prayer and suddenly found herself, without knowing how, carried body and soul into Hell. She says she instantly understood that God wished her to see the place she would have occupied if not for her conversion. No words can relate the vision of suffering she saw in Hell. It was, St. Teresa said, beyond human comprehension.

In her *Autobiography*, St. Teresa explains that there was "no light" in Hell, that it was an "eternal pit, only darkness of the deepest dye: and yet although there was no light, all the torments of Hell could be perceived." The great saint said she felt in her soul a devouring fire and that her body was prey to intolerable pains. Nothing in her lifetime could compare to it, she insisted, despite the many sufferings she had incurred.

Teresa confirmed other traditional beliefs concerning Hell. There was, she remembered, a "pestiferous odor" by which one was continually "suffocated" and numerous distressing sights. The hottest fire of this world could not compare, she asserted. It was like comparing "a painted fire with the fire of Hell." Most of all, Teresa emphasized that she was given to understand such suffering was, indeed, "unending and unalleviated."

But although the tortures of the senses were unbearable, she concluded that they were nothing in comparison to the anguish of the soul: "While I felt myself burned, and as if hacked into a thousand pieces, I was suffering all the agonies of death, all the horrors of despair. There was not a particle of hope, of consolation, in this frightening sojourn."

In short, St. Teresa admitted that what she was shown was worse than anything she had read about Hell in books. Ten years after her vision of Hell, Teresa confessed she was still seized with terror over its memory, yet she used the experience to draw strength and bear up under her own trials and sufferings.

St. Teresa is not alone in her experience. St. Bernard related a vision of Hell that a fellow priest had experienced. Like St. Teresa, Bernard would later explain that the horrors were something no one would want to see yet were used to strengthen the religious in their trials.

Similarly, St. John Damasene recounts the story of St. Josephat. Praying to God one day, St. Josephat asked that he be delivered from his temptations. His prayer was heard as he was caught up into ecstasy and found himself in a dark place filled with confusion, horror, and frightful sights. He then saw a pool of fire and sulphur in which were "plunged" innumerable souls. From out of the flames, howls, and shouts, he heard a "heavenly voice" say, "Here it is that sin receives its punishment; here it is that a moment's pleasure is punished by an eternity of torments." Like St. Teresa and St. Bernard, St. Josephat said the vision gave him "new" strength in order to help him defeat the assaults of the enemy in his own life.

While "visions of Hell" and "apparitions of the damned" have been reported for two thousand years or more, the revelations of the last two centuries appear to provide something more. Many of these reported accounts of Hell, like the preceding ones, not only continue to confirm the existence of Hell and its horrors, but they also offer a prophetic picture of our present times. It is a picture that not only reveals an escalation in the ongoing war between Heaven and Hell in the past two centuries, but it also strongly suggests that this war is nearing a climax.

Therefore, in the next chapter, we will look not only at the descriptions and accounts of those shown Hell in more modern times, but also at some of the accompanying revelations to help illuminate our Christian understanding of what St. Paul so clearly conveyed: we are all part of a war "against the principalities and powers, with the rulers of the world, of this present darkness" (Eph 6:12).

CHAPTER THIRTEEN

HELL UNLEASHED

The "Age of Mary," beginning in the early 19th century and extending to the present, has proven to be fertile ground for private revelations concerning Hell. Similar to previous "visions of hell" and "apparitions of the damned," many are graphic and indeed, frightening. However, some of these revelations involve not only descriptions of Hell and visits from the damned, but a more clearly defined picture of the activities and inhabitants of Hell. Recent mystics have disclosed that a great spiritual war is unfolding in the world, resulting in the loss of many souls. Consequently, the visions serve to warn the faithful in a profoundly new way that Hell is a very real threat to souls, perhaps more than ever before.

Venerable Anna Catherine Emmerich, the most celebrated of the 18th century Catholic mystics, reported not only traditional perceptions of Hell—a horrid, fiery abyss of misery filled with the unrepentant—but also a warning that the demons of the underworld were being "loosed" on mankind in an unprecedented way. Emmerich was given to understand that time had reached its fullness in a way foretold in Scripture long ago. And with this fullness, came a decisive confrontation between Heaven and Hell—a confrontation destined to fulfill many prophecies:

> At last I saw Him, His countenance grace and severe, approaching the center of the abyss, namely, hell itself. In shape it looked to me like an immeasurably vast, frightful, black stone building that shone with a metallic lustre. Its entrance was guarded by immense,

awful-looking doors, black like the rest of the building, ad furnished with bolts and locks that inspired feelings of terror. Roaring and yelling most horribly could plainly be heard, and when the doors were pushed open, a frightful gloomy world was disclosed to view.

As I am accustomed to see the heavenly Jerusalem under the form of a city, and the abodes of the blessed therein under various kinds of palaces and gardens full of wonderful fruits and flowers, all according to the different degrees of glory, so here I saw everything under the appearance of a world whose buildings, open spaces, and various regions were all closely connected. But all proceeded from the opposite of happiness, all was pain and torment. As in the sojourns of the blessed, all appears formed upon motives and conditions of infinite peace, eternal harmony and satisfaction, so here are the disorder, the malformation of eternal wrath, disunion, and despair.

As in heaven there are innumerable abodes of joy and worship, unspeakably beautiful in their glittering transparency, so here in hell, are gloomy prisons without number, caves of torment, of cursing, and despair. As in heaven there are gardens most wonderful to behold, filled with fruits that afford divine nourishment, so here in hell, there are horrible wildernesses and swamps full of torture and pain and of all that can give birth to feelings of detestation, of loathing, and of horror. I saw here temples, altars, palaces, thrones, gardens, lakes, streams, all formed of blasphemy, hatred, cruelty, despair, confusion, pain, and torture, while in heaven all is built up of benedictions, of love, harmony, joy, and delight. *Here* is the rending, eternal disunion of the damned; *there* is the blissful communion of the saints. All the roots of perversity and untruth are here cultivated in countless forms and deeds of punishment and affliction. Nothing here is right, no thought brings peace, for the terrible remembrance of divine justice casts every damned soul into the pain and torment that his own guilt has planted for him. All that is terrible here both in appearance and reality, is the nature, the form, the fury of sin unmasked, the serpent, that now flourishes. I saw there also frightful columns erected for the sole purpose of creating feelings of horror and terror, just as in the Kingdom of God they are intended to inspire peace and the sentiment of blissful rest, etc. All this is easily understood, but cannot be expressed in detail.

When the gates were swung open by the angels, one beheld before him a struggling, blaspheming, mocking, howling, and lamenting throng. I saw that Jesus spoke some words to the soul of Judas. Some of the angels forced that multitude of evil spirits to prostrate before Jesus, for all had to acknowledge and adore Him. This was for them the most terrible torment. A great number were chained in a circle around others who were in turn bound down by them. In the centre was an abyss of darkness. Lucifer was cast into it, chained, and thick black vapor mounted up around him. This took place by the Divine Decree. I heard that Lucifer (if I do not mistake) will be freed again for awhile fifty or sixty years before the year 2000 AD. I have forgotten many other dates that were told me. Some other demons are to be freed before Lucifer, in order to chastise and tempt mankind. I think that some are let loose now in our own day, and others will be freed shortly after our time.

Emmerich's revelations of Hell were echoed by other mystics of her day. The celebrated stigmatist Elizabeth Canori-Mora claimed she saw Hell, too, and that it was being unleashed upon the world: "God will allow the demons to strike with death those impious men because they gave themselves up to the inferring powers—great legions of devils shall roam the whole earth, leaving a trail of ruins."

The visions of another mystic of the era, Blessed Anna Marie Taigi, are also closely aligned with those of Emmerich and Canori-Mora. Taigi, too, was shown that many souls, including those of religious, were going to Hell. Souls were "falling into hell like snowflakes," she said, where they "wept and sobbed in bitterness." In one vision, Taigi saw laymen falling into the abyss, likewise ecclesiastical dignitaries, priests, and men and women of religious orders. "The air will be infested with demons," said Taigi, "who will appear under hideous forms."

By the time Mary appeared at Ru due Bac, Paris, in 1830, more visions and revelations concerning Hell were emerging. At Ru due Bac, Mary spoke of the war underway between Heaven and Hell, and that the loss of many souls was at stake—souls headed for damnation. A little more than a decade later, the Virgin further defined the situation. In 1846 at La Salette, France, Mary revealed that historic times were at hand. Her great, apocalyptic prophecy specifically concerned Hell and its reality: Souls are being "plunged for eternity...into the everlasting chains of Hell," she said, and "Lucifer, with a large number of demons, will put an end to faith little by little."

By the mid-19th century, even more revelations of Hell were being reported. St. John Vianney, a parish priest in the village of Ars, France, had profound experiences of Hell and its inhabitants. Likewise, so did Maria Julie Jahenney, a stigmatist from Blain who spoke about the "Halls of Hell." At Pompeii, Italy, in 1872, the Virgin Mary told Blessed Bartolo Longo that if he wanted to be saved "from going to Hell," he should spread devotion to the Rosary. Nearly twenty years later, the messages given to two little girls (Cellesia Passi, 14, and Perpetua Lorenzi, 13) at Campetello, Corsica, were the same. "Pray," Mary beseeched the children, and tell the village people to pray as well, so they will "not to go to Hell."

One account of Hell from this era is especially worth noting. St. John Bosco reportedly visited the bowels of Hell where he saw souls smothered with worms and vermin gnawing at their bodies, as well as chastising fires pouring forth from dark caves and crevices. Don Bosco's dream is described and its purpose discussed in *To Hell and Back*:

> "Do you really believe that some of them would reform if you were to warn them? Then and there your warning might impress them, but soon they will forget it saying, 'It was just a dream,' and they will do worse than before. Others, realizing they have been

unmasked, will receive the sacraments, but this will be neither spontaneous nor meritorious; others will go to confession because of a momentary fear of hell but will still be attached to sin."

"Then is there no way to save these unfortunate lads? Please, tell me what I can do for them."

"They have superiors; let them obey them. They have rules; let them observe them. They have the sacraments; let them receive them."

Just then a new group of boys came hurtling down and the portals momentarily opened. "Let's go in," the guide said to me.

I pulled back in horror. I could not wait to rush back to the Oratory to warn the boys, lest others might be lost as well.

"Come," my guide insisted. "You'll learn much. But first tell me: Do you wish to go alone or with me?" He asked this to make me realize that I was not brave enough and therefore needed his friendly assistance.

"Alone inside that horrible place?" I replied. *"How will I ever be able to find my way our without our help?"* Then a thought came to my mind and aroused my courage. *Before one is condemned to hell,* I said to myself, *he must be judged. And I haven't been judged yet!*

"Let's go," I exclaimed resolutely. We entered that narrow, horrible corridor and whizzed through it with lightening speed. Threatening inscriptions shone eerily over all the inner gateways. The last one opened into a vast, grim courtyard with a large, unbelievably forbidding entrance at the far end. Above it stood this inscription:

"Those will go off to eternal punishment." (Mt 25:46) The walls all about were similarly inscribed. I asked my guide if I could read them, and he consented. These were the inscriptions. "He will send fire and worms into their flesh, and they shall burn and suffer forever" (Jud 16:17). There they will be tortured day and night forever and ever" (Rev 20:10). "...and the smoke of their torment shall rise forever and ever" (Rev 14:11). "...the black, disordered land where darkness is the only light" (Job 10:22). "There is no peace for the wicked." (Is 48:22) "Wailing will be heard there, and the grinding of teeth" (Mt 8:12).

While I moved from one inscription to another, my guide, who had stood in the center of the courtyard, came up to me. "From here on," he said, "no one may have a helpful companion, a comforting friend, a loving heart, a compassionate glance, or a benevolent word. All this is gone forever. Do you just want to see or would you rather experience these things yourself?"

"I only want to see!" I answered.

"Then come with me," my friend added, and, taking me in tow, he stepped through that gate into a corridor at whose far end stood an observation platform, closed by a huge, single crystal pane reaching from the pavement to the ceiling. As soon as I crossed its threshold, I felt an indescribable terror and dared not take another step. Ahead of me I could see something like an immense cave which gradually disappeared into recesses sunk far into the bowels of the mountains. They were all ablaze, but theirs was not an earthly fire with leaping tongues of flames. The entire cave-walls, ceiling floor, iron, stones, wood, and coal-everything was a glowing white at temperatures of thousands of degrees. Yet the fire did not incinerate, did not consume. I simply can't find words to describe the cavern's horror. "Broad and deep, it is piled with dry grass and wood in abundance. And the breath of the Lord, like a stream of sulfur, will set it afire." (Is 30:33)

I was staring in bewilderment about me when a lad dashed out of a gate. Seemingly unaware of anything else, he emitted a most shrilling scream, like one who is about to fall into a cauldron of liquid bronze, and plummeted into the center of the cave. Instantly he too became incandescent and perfectly motionless, while the echo of his dying wail lingered for an instant more.

Terribly frightened, I stared briefly at him for a while. He seemed to be one of my Oratory boys. *"Isn't he so and so?"* I asked my guide.

"Yes," was the answer.

"Why is he so still, so incandescent?"

"You choose to see," he replied. "Be satisfied with that. Just keep looking. Besides, 'everyone will be salted with fire'" (Mk 9:49).

As I looked again, another boy came hurtling down into the cave at breakneck speed. He too was from the Oratory. As he fell, so he remained. He too emitted one single heart-rending shriek that blended with the last echo of the scream that came from the youth who had preceded him. Other boys kept hurtling in the same way in increasing numbers, all screaming the same way and then all becoming equally motionless and incandescent. I noticed that the first seemed frozen to the spot, one hand and one foot raised into the air; the second boy seemed bent almost double to the floor. Others stood or hung in various other positions, balancing themselves on one foot or hand, sitting or lying on their backs or on their sides, standing or kneeling, hands clutching their hair. Briefly, the scene resembled a large statuary group of youngsters cast into ever more painful postures. Other lads hurtled into that same furnace. Some I knew; others were strangers to me. I then recalled what is written in the Bible to the effect that as one falls into hell, so he shall forever remain "....wherever it falls, there shall it lie" (Eccles 11:3).

More frightened than ever, I asked my guide, *"When these boys come dashing into this cave, don't they know where they are going?"*

"They surely do. They have been warned a thousand times, but they still choose to rush into the fire because they do not detest sin and are loath to forsake it. Furthermore, they despise and reject God's incessant, merciful invitations to do penance. Thus provoked,

Divine Justice harries them, hounds them, and goads them on so that they cannot halt until they reach this place."

"Oh, how miserable these unfortunate boys must feel in knowing they no longer have any hope," I exclaimed.

"If you really want to know their innermost frenzy and fury, go a little closer," my guide remarked.

I took a few steps forward and saw that many of those poor wretches were savagely striking at each other like mad dogs. Others were clawing their own faces and hands, tearing their own flesh and spitefully throwing it about. Just then, the entire ceiling of the cave became as transparent as crystal and revealed a patch of heaven and their radiant companions safe for all eternity.

The poor wretches, fuming and panting with envy, burned with rage because they had once ridiculed the just. "The wicked man shall see it and be vexed; he shall gnash his teeth and pine away..." (Ps 112:10).

"Why do I hear no sound?" I asked my guide.

"Go closer!" he advised.

Pressing my ear to the crystal window, I heard screams and sobs, blasphemies and imprecations against the saints. It was a tumult of voices and cries, shrill and confused.

"When they recall the happy lot of their good companions," he replied, "they are obliged to admit: "His life we accounted to madness, and his death dishonored. See how he is accounted among the sons of God; and how his lot is with the saints! We, then, have strayed from the way of truth..." (Wis 5:4-6).

"Such are the mournful chants which shall echo here throughout eternity. But their shouts, their efforts and their cries are all in vain...terrors shall fall upon them" (Job 20:25).

"Here time is no more. Here is only eternity."

While I viewed the condition of many of my boys in utter terror, a thought suddenly struck me. *"How can these boys be damned?"* I asked. *"Last night they were still alive at the Oratory!"*

"The boys you see here," he answered, "are all dead to God's grace. Were they to die now or persist in their evil ways, they would be damned. But we are wasting time. Let us go on."

He led me away and we went down through a corridor into a lower cavern, at whose entrance I read: "Their worm shall not die, nor their fire be extinguished" (Is 66:24). "He will send fire and worms into their flesh, and they shall burn and suffer" (Jud 16:17).

Here one could see how atrocious was the remorse of those who had been pupils in our schools. What a torment was theirs to remember each unforgiven sin and its just punishment, the countless, even extraordinary means they had had to mend their ways, persevere in virtue, and earn paradise, and their lack of response to many favors promised and bestowed by the Virgin Mary. What a torture to think that they could have been saved so easily, yet now are irredeemably lost, and to remember the many good resolutions made and never kept. Hell is indeed paved with good intentions!

In this lower cavern I again saw those Oratory boys who had fallen into the fiery furnace. Some are listening to me right now; others are former pupils or even strangers to me. I drew closer to them and noticed that they were all covered with worms and vermin which gnawed at their vitals, hears, eyes, hands, legs, and entire bodies so ferociously as to defy description. Helpless and motionless, they were a prey to every kind of torment. Hoping I might be able to speak with them or to hear something from them, I drew even closer but no one spoke or even looked at me. I then asked my guide why, and he explained that the damned are totally deprived of freedom. Each must fully endure his own punishment, with absolutely no reprieve whatever.

By the early 20th century, an even better understanding of Hell and what was unfolding in the world emerged. At Fatima in 1917, the Virgin Mary appeared to three children for six months. A profound vision of Hell was given to the visionaries, one as vivid and descriptive as any ever recorded in the annals of private revelation. Thirteen years later, the Church approved the events of Fatima, and indirectly stamped this account of Hell with its imprimatur, setting the stage for a century of more such revelations of the damned and the dangerous times that were now at hand.

CHAPTER FOURTEEN

GOD WANTS TO SAVE SOULS

A s with the 19th century revelations of Hell, many of those in the 20th century involve prophecies concerning the seriousness our times. The visionaries report that sin is epidemic today, and that this is leading to (1) the danger of an earthly chastisement, to be permitted by God for the sins of the world, and, (2) the danger of many souls going to Hell, as an eternal consequence of the ocean of evil that is inundating the world.

This book is not about the prophecies of the spiritual war at hand, but needless to say, many 20th century revelations of Hell appear to be linked to these prophecies, making it difficult to separate the two themes. Moreover, this linkage seems to be intended by God. In this regard, Pope Leo XIII's 1884 vision of a great war erupting between Heaven and Hell during the 20th century seems only too relevant for our times.

Many extraordinary revelations of Hell occurred during the early 20th century. A victim soul named Marthe Robin, reported her experiences with Hell and its occupants, as did Padre Pio, the Italian mystic, whose accounts of Hell and its demons were more frightening than his revelations of Purgatory. Padre Pio even claimed to have been physically attacked by the devil. In France, another "Cure of Ars" figure, named Père Lamy, emerged at the beginning of the century with prophecies and visions that are still well-read today.

Père Lamy

This French priest and visionary reported that the Virgin Mary showed him the infernal regions and its leader, Lucifer; who was dressed, said Fr. Lamy, "in the fires of Hell":

> Lucifer is tall, with quite a good-looking face, bony, bearded. He has fierce eyes, flashing; light hair, a fairly short, curly beard. He has the build of a very solid man of strong cut. He wears a white garment, a sort of antique peplum which comes halfway down his leg. Always climbing zig-zag the length of his body and his robe, through his beard, from the feet to the top of his head, are two kinds of flames which seem to stick to him. One kind, the most numerous, are black as burning pitch. The other are ordinary tongues of fire, like the fire of that lamp over there. He suffers in silence and makes no outcry. It does not hinder his movements. The Blessed Virgin shows him to me in his sufferings: and this deprives him of any authority. When I see him surrounded with flames, or rather, when the Blessed Virgin has the goodness to let me see his face surrounded with flames, I reckon the sufferings of Lucifer dreadful, dreadful....

Fatima

From the Virgin Mary's apparitions at Fatima in 1917 has come the century's most powerful private revelation. On July 13th, the Virgin Mary appeared to three shepherd children at Fatima's Cova da Iria (Hollow of Irene) for the third time. In answer to the oldest visionary, Lucia dos Santó, the Virgin Mary promised that in October she would work a great miracle, "so that all might believe." After revealing this, Mary told the children to sacrifice themselves for sinners and to say, many times, a prayer she taught them.

Then, while speaking, the Virgin held out her hands, from which emanated bright rays that appeared to penetrate the earth. Suddenly, the ground vanished and the children found themselves standing on the edge of a sea of fire. As they stared into the vast lake of molten liquid, they saw a great number of devils and damned souls. The demons resembled black animals, each filling the air with shrieks, screams, and moaning cries. The souls, Lucia would later write, appeared to be in their bodies, rolling and trembling helplessly in the flames. They had no peace, even for a moment, and were constantly in pain, said Lucia. "You have seen Hell," Mary then told the children, "where the souls of sinners go."

Sister Lucia, in several of her Memoirs, detailed this horrifying vision. In the *First Memoir* (1935), she provided the following description:

> That day, when we reached the pasture, Jacinta sat thoughtfully on a rock.
>
> "Jacinta, come and play."
>
> "I don't want to play today."
>
> "Why not?"
>
> "Because I'm thinking. The Lady told us to say the Rosary and to make sacrifices for the conversion of sinners. So from now on, when we say the Rosary we must say the whole Hail Mary and the whole Our Father! And the sacrifices, how are we going to make them?"
>
> Right away, Francisco thought of a good sacrifice: "Let's give our lunch to the sheep, and make the sacrifice of doing without it."
>
> In a couple of minutes, the contents of our lunch bag had been divided among the sheep. So that day, we fasted as strictly as the most austere Carthusian! Jacinta remained sitting on her rock, looking very thoughtful, and asked: "The Lady also said that many souls go to hell! What is hell, then?"
>
> "It's like a big deep pit of wild beasts, with an enormous fire in it— that's how my mother used to explain it to me—and that's where people go who commit sins and don't confess them. They stay there and burn forever!"
>
> "And they never get out of there again?"
>
> "No!"
>
> "Not even after many, many years?"
>
> "No! Hell never ends!"
>
> "And heaven never ends either?"
>
> "Whoever goes to heaven, never leaves it again!"
>
> "And whoever goes to hell, never leaves it either?"
>
> "They're eternal, don't you see! They never

end."

That was how, for the first time, we made a meditation on hell and eternity. What made the biggest impression on Jacinta was the idea of eternity. Even in the middle of a game, she would stop and ask: "But listen! Doesn't hell end after many, many years then?"

Or again: "Those people burning in hell, don't they ever die? And don't they turn into ashes? And if people pray very much for sinners, won't Our Lord get them out of there? And if they make sacrifices as well? Poor sinners! We have to pray and make many sacrifices for them!"

Then she went on: "How good the Lady is! She has already promised to take us to heaven!"

*

In her *Third Memoir* (1941), Sr. Lucia provided an even more profound account of the vision of Hell:

Well, the secret is made up of three distinct parts, two of which I am going to reveal. The first part is the vision of hell. Our Lady showed us a great sea of fire which seemed to be under the earth. Plunged in this fire were demons and souls in human form, like transparent burning embers, all blackened or burnished bronze, floating about in the conflagration, now raised into the air by the flames that issued from within themselves together with great clouds of smoke, now falling back on every side like sparks in a huge fire, without weight or equilibrium, and amid shrieks and groans of pain and despair, which horrified us and made us tremble with fear. The demons could be distinguished by their terrifying and repellent likeness to frightful and unknown animals, all black and transparent. This vision lasted but an instant. How can we ever be grateful enough to our kind heavenly Mother, who had already prepared us by promising in the first apparition, to take us to heaven. Otherwise, I think we would have died of fear and terror.

We then looked up at Our Lady, who said to us so kindly and so sadly: "You have seen hell where the souls of poor sinners go. To save them, God wishes to establish in the world devotion to my Immaculate Heart. If what I say to you is done, many souls will be saved and there will be peace. The war is going to end: but if people do not cease offending God, a worse one will break out during the pontificate of Pius XI. When you see a night illumined by an unknown light, know that this is the great sign given you by God that He is about to punish the world for its crimes, by means of war, famine, and persecutions of the Church and of the Holy Father.

"To prevent this, I shall come to ask for the consecration of Russia to my Immaculate Heart, and the Communion of reparation on the First Saturdays. If my requests are heeded. Russia will be converted, and there will be peace: if not, she will spread her errors throughout the world, causing wars and persecutions of the Church. The good will be martyred; the Holy Father will have much to suffer; various nations will be annihilated. In the end, my Immaculate Heart will triumph. The Holy Father will consecrate Russia to me, and she will be converted, and a period of peace will be granted to the world."

★

In Sr. Lucia's *Fourth Memoir* (1941), she elaborated further on the vision of Hell with regard to Francisco Marto's vision of the devil:

How different is the incident that I now call to mind. One day we went to a place called Pedreira, and while the sheep were browsing, we jumped from rock to rock, making our voices echo down in the deep ravines. Francisco withdrew, as was his wont, to a hollow among the rocks.

A considerable time had elapsed, when we heard

him shouting and crying out to us and to Our Lady. Distressed lest something might have happened to him, we ran in search of him, calling out his name.

"Where are you?"

"Here! Here!"

But it still took us some time before we could locate him. At last, we came upon him, trembling with fright, still on his knees, and so upset that he was unable to rise to his feet.

"What's wrong? What happened to you?"

In a voice half smothered with fright, he replied: "It was one of those huge beasts that we saw in hell. He was right here breathing out flames!"

I saw nothing, neither did Jacinta, so I laughed and said to him: "You never want to think about hell, so as not to be afraid; and now you're the first one to be frightened!"

Indeed, whenever Jacinta appeared particularly moved by the remembrance of hell, he used to say to her: "Don't think so much about hell! Think about Our Lord and Our Lady instead. I don't think about hell, so as not to be afraid."

He was anything but fearful. He'd go anywhere in the dark alone at night without the lightest hesitation. He played with lizards, and when he came across any snakes, he got them to entwine themselves round a stick, and even poured sheep's milk into the holes in the rocks for them to drink. He went hunting for foxes' holes and rabbits' burrows, and other creatures of the wilds.

★

Fatima writers have often alluded to how strongly affected Jacinta was by her experience of Hell. Indeed, although only a child, her great spirituality has often been attributed to the effects of the vision. Sr. Lucia commented on these effects in her *Third Memoir.*

Your Excellency, as I already told you in the notes I sent to you after reading the book about Jacinta, some of

the things revealed in the secret made a very strong
impression on her. This was indeed the case. The vision
of hell filled her with horror to such a degree, that every
penance and modification was as nothing in her eyes, if it
could only prevent souls from going there.

Well, I am going to answer the second question,
one which has come to me from various quarters.

How is it that Jacinta, small as she was, let herself
be possessed by such a spirit of mortification and penance,
and understood it so well?

I think the reason is this: firstly, God willed to
bestow on her a special grace, through the Immaculate
Heart of Mary; and secondly, it was because she had
looked upon hell, and had seen the ruin of souls who fall
therein.

Some people, even the most devout, refuse to
speak to children about hell, in case it would frighten
them. Yet God did not hesitate to show hell to three
children, one of whom was only six years old, knowing
well that they would be horrified to the point of, I would
almost dare to say, withering away from fear.

Jacinta often sat thoughtfully on the ground or on
a rock, and exclaimed:

"Oh, Hell! Hell! How sorry I am for the souls
who go to hell! And the people down there, burning alive,
like wood in the fire!" Then, shuddering, she knelt down
with her hands joined, and recited the prayer that Our
Lady had taught us:

"O my Jesus! Forgive us, save us from the fire of
hell. Lead all souls to heaven, especially those who are
most in need."

Now Your Excellency will understand how my
own impression was that the final words of this prayer refer
to souls in greatest danger of damnation, or those who are
nearest to it. Jacinta remained on her knees like this for
long periods of time, saying the same prayer over and over
again. From time to time, like someone awaking from
sleep, she called out to her brother or myself:

"Francisco! Francisco! Are you praying with me? We must pray very much, to save souls from hell! So many go there! So many!" At other times, she asked: "Why doesn't Our Lady show hell to sinners? If they saw it, they would not sin, so as to avoid going there! You must tell Our Lady to show hell to all the people (referring to those who were in the Cova da Iria at the time of the Apparition). You'll see how they will be converted."

Afterwards, unsatisfied, she asked me: "Why didn't you tell Our Lady to show hell to those people?"

"I forgot," I answered.

"I didn't remember either!" she said, looking very sad.

Sometimes, she also asked: "What are the sins people commit, for which they go to hell?"

"I don't know! Perhaps the sin of not going to Mass on Sunday, of stealing, of saying ugly words, of cursing and of swearing."

"So for just one word, then, people can go to hell?"

"Well, it's a sin!"

"It wouldn't be hard for them to keep quiet, and to go to Mass! I'm so sorry for sinners! If only I could show them hell!"

Suddenly, she would seize hold of me and say:

"I'm going to heaven, but you are staying here. If Our Lady lets you, tell everybody what hell is like, so that they won't commit any more sins and not go to hell."

At other times, after thinking for a while, she said: "So many people falling into hell! So many people in hell!"

To quiet her, I said: "Don't be afraid! You're going to heaven."

"Yes, I am," she said serenely, "but I want all those people to go there, too!"

When, in a spirit of mortification, she did not want to eat, I said to her:

"Listen, Jacinta! Come and eat now."

"No! I'm offering this sacrifice for sinners who eat too much."

When she was ill, and yet went to Mass on a week day, I urged her:

"Jacinta, don't come! You can't, you're not able. Besides, today is not a Sunday!"

"That doesn't matter! I'm going for sinners who don't go on Sunday."

If she happened to hear any of those expressions which some people make a show of uttering, she covered her face with her hands and said:

"Oh, my God, don't those people realize that they can go to hell for saying those things? My Jesus, forgive them and convert them. They certainly don't know that they are offending God by all this! What a pity, my Jesus! I'll pray for them." There and then, she repeated the prayer that Our Lady had taught us: "Oh, my Jesus, forgive us...."

Sr. Josefa Menendez

Not long after Fatima, in 1922, another extraordinary revelation on Hell was granted to Sr. Josefa Menendez, a sister of the Society of the Sacred Heart, who lived in a convent in Portiers, France. Sr. Menendez's revelations were unique, for the nun claimed actual visitations to Hell:

On the night of March 16th, towards ten o'clock....I became aware, as on the preceding days, of a confused noise of cries and chains. I rose quickly and dressed, and trembling with fright, knelt down near my bed. The uproar was approaching, and not knowing what to do, I left the dormitory, and went to our Holy Mother's cell; then I came back to the dormitory. The same terrifying sounds were all round me; then all of a sudden I saw in front of me the devil himself.

"'Tie her feet and bind her hands,' he cried....

Instantly I lost sight of where I was, and felt myself tightly bound and being dragged away. Other voices screamed: "No good to bind her feet; it is her heart that you must bind."

"'It does not belong to me,' came the answer from the devil.

Then I was dragged along a very dark and lengthy passage, and on all sides resounded terrible cries. On opposite sides of the walls of this narrow corridor were niches out of which poured smoke with very little flame, and which emitted an intolerable stench. From these recesses came blaspheming voices, uttering impure words. Some cursed their bodies, others their parents. Others, again reproached themselves having refused grace, and not avoiding what they knew to be sinful. It was a torrent of confused screams of rage and despair. I was dragged through that kind of corridor, which seemed endless.

Then I received a violent punch which doubled me in two, and forced me into one of the niches. I felt as if I were being passed between two burning planks and pierced through and through with scorching needle points. Opposite and beside me souls were blaspheming and cursing me. What caused me the most suffering...and with which no torture can be compared, was the anguish of my soul to find myself separated from God...

It seemed to me that I spent long years in that hell, yet it lasted only six or seven hours....Suddenly I was violently pulled out of the niche, and I found myself in a dark place. After striking me, the devil disappeared and left me free.... How can I describe my feelings on realizing that I was still alive, and could still love God!

I do not know what I am not ready to endure to avoid hell, in spite of my fear of pain. I see clearly that all the sufferings of earth are nothing in comparison with the horror of no longer being able to love, for in that place all breathes hatred and thirst to damn other souls.

★

Josefa described this moment of transport in words of passionate fervor:

On Sunday, 19th March 1922, which was the third Sunday of Lent, I once more went down into the abyss, and it seemed to me that I remained there for long years. I suffered much, but the greatest of my torments was in believing that I could no longer love Our Lord. When I come back to life I am simply mad with joy. I think my love has increased tenfold and I feel ready to endure for love of Him whatever He wishes. As to my vocation, I esteem and love it to folly!

What I have seen gives me great courage to suffer, and makes me understand the value of the smallest sacrifices; Jesus gathers them up and uses them to save souls. It is blindness to avoid pain even in very small things, for not only is it of great worth to ourselves, but it serves to guard many from the torments of hell.

On Sunday, 26th March, Sr. Josefa detailed the distress of her experience:

On reaching that abode of horror, I hear yells of rage and devilish exultation because another soul has fallen into everlasting torments.....

At the moment I am not conscious of having previously gone down into hell; it always seems to me the first time. It seems, too, to be forever, and what an agony that is, for I remember that I once knew and loved Our Lord.... that I was a religious, that He conferred great graces on me, and many means by which to save my soul. What was it, then, that I did? How did I come to lose so many good things?...How should I have been so blind?...And now all hope is gone...My communions, too, come back to my mind, and my novitiate. But the most crushing and overwhelming grief of all is the tormenting memory that I once loved the Heart of Jesus so dearly. I knew Him and He was everything to me

Him....

It is impossible to put into words the poignant distress to which my broken and oppressed soul is reduced....

Sr. Faustina Kowalska

During the 1930's, another victim soul recorded revelations of Hell. Sister Faustina Kowalska noted in her famous *Diary* how God showed her Hell:

> Today, I was led by an Angel to the chasms of hell. It is a place of great torture; how awesomely large and extensive it is! The kinds of tortures I saw: the first torture that constitutes hell is the loss of God; the second is perpetual remorse of conscience; the third is that one's condition will never change; the fourth is the fire that will penetrate the soul without destroying it—a terrible suffering, since it is a purely spiritual fire, lit by God's anger; the fifth torture is continual darkness, the devils and the souls of the damned see each other and all the evil, both of others and their own; the sixth torture is the constant company of Satan; the seventh torture is horrible despair, hatred of God, vile words, curses and blasphemies.
>
> These are the tortures suffered by all the damned together, but that is not the end of the sufferings. There are special tortures destined for particular souls. These are the torments of the senses. Each soul undergoes terrible and indescribable sufferings, related to the manner in which it has sinned. There are caverns and pits of torture where one firm of agony differs from another. I would have died at the very sight of these tortures if the omnipotence of God had not supported me. Let the sinner know that he will be tortured throughout all eternity, in those senses which were made use of to sin. I am writing this at the command of God, so that no soul may find an excuse by saying there is no hell, or that nobody has ever been there, and that no one can say what

it is like.

I, Sister Faustina, by the order of God, have visited the abysses of hell so that I might tell souls about it and testify to its existence. I cannot speak about it now; but I have received a command from God to leave it in writing. The devils were full of hatred for me, but they had to obey me at the command of God. What I have written is but a pale shadow of the things I saw. But I noticed one thing: that most of the souls there are those who disbelieved that there is a hell. When I came to, I could hardly recover from the fright. How terribly souls suffer there! Consequently, I pray even more fervently for the conversion of sinners. I incessantly plead God's mercy upon them. O my Jesus, I would rather be in agony until the end of the world, amidst the greatest sufferings, than offend You by the least sin.

In this latter half of the 20th century, more visions and revelations of Hell have been reported. As before, many are from personal experiences. It would not be possible to write of them all, but the revelations of Christina Gallagher, in particular, deserve attention.

Christina Gallagher

The following account is excerpted from the author's book, *The Sorrow, The Sacrifice, and the Triumph: The Apparitions, Visions, and Prophecies of Christina Gallagher.*

Christina Gallagher reveals the same recurring nightmare. On March 29, 1989, Jesus showed Christina Hell. It was gripping. "Terrifying," she says. A miserable sight. She says she gazed at a sea of fire spread across a vast area. "Hell," she said, "was so enormous."

This huge area, filled with bursting flames, held many helpless people. They were immersed in the flames and their bodies appeared in "different shapes and black in color." Christina watched these bodies go in and out of the flames, suffering to the extent that it was "unbearable to watch." The flames, she concluded, seemed to be "going through them."

After seeing Hell, Our Lord told her, "This is the abyss of sin; Hell for all those who do not love My Father. My daughter, unite your weakness with Me Who is all strength."

For Christina, like Lucia, Hell was unforgettable.

" Hell, was just total fire, Jesus was with me through the whole experience. It was a terrifying experience beyond words; I never want to experience it again. It was a great darkness and very frightening. All I could see was an endless sea of fire, and somehow I could look down through it, with enormous flames going into flames. And there were the shapes of bodies in it, as if in a sea, swimming in this fire. The bodies were black and the intense flames were going through them. I could look down through the flames. There was an enormous amount of bodies. I felt an awful sense of terror. I could do nothing but quiver. I pray nobody will ever have to go to Hell."

Her intercession to save thousands of souls from Hell has already been sought. Once, after five weeks of suffering, she was invited to surrender to crucifixion.

Christina complied, telling the Lord, "If necessary, crucify me."

After this, she witnessed the appearance of many angry demons. The next day, Jesus informed her that through her suffering, five thousand souls were saved from the brink of Hell; those souls were still alive, Jesus explained to her. When Christina inquired, "What if they go back to their sinful ways?" Jesus replied, "I have touched them in such a way that they will be spiritually saved and healed in eternal life."

Like many of the saints, Christina says those who go to Hell choose this fate—reasoning that goes against all logic, but it is true.

"As I understand it, it has to do with free will and sin," says Christina. "You know, some people are not aware that they're committing sin. That's where the pastors of any Church must come in. They are to make people aware of the reality of sin. So many people don't recognize sin. But God is Mercy and God is so full of love that people who are not aware of sin may go through a great suffering to make themselves aware. It's like a purification. God desires salvation for everyone but it's entirely up to man to come and seek God's helping hand. If they do, that's fine.

There are those who decide they know they are doing wrong and still have no intentions of changing their ways. These people may want everything of the world in preference to God—power and luxury—and they know it's wrong. Consciously, they are aware of it and they know they are serving the Devil. He's the prince or the king of this world. This is his kingdom—this world. I now realize how the flesh tempts us. The flesh is weak. We must turn to God and beg God for His grace through prayer and the sacraments. We must decrease in self and permit the Spirit of God to increase."

"Prayer, fasting, and all that we can offer up is what God is asking us to do. God is giving us strength through His grace, through prayer, and through the sacraments. When man intentionally turns away from God and doesn't want to know Him, then he must clearly understand the road he's on is the road to hell. Yes, man therefore chooses Hell himself by his actions."

After the shocking scene of Hell, the Blessed Mother again offered Christina encouragement. Our Lady reminded her of the sad state of affairs the world was in. It is a world, said the Virgin, where many more souls are going to go to Hell if the messages continue to be unheeded. "My daughter, do not be afraid of those of the world. Put all in the world beneath your feet, and work only for Salvation. The Purification is close at hand. Many will be lost for the sins of the world and the sins of the flesh. You, my daughter, must make reparation for those who talk in blasphemy about my Son in the See of Peter. My

Son is surrounded by many whose hearts are full of hate and jealousy."

In late October 1992, with the experience of Hell still stamped in Christina's memory, the Queen of Peace again pleaded:

There are many calamities to come to the world. The soul of humanity will be cleansed. God desires that I come to many parts of the world to warn my children. Some respond for a time, others do not want to know me. There are many who will go to Hell. The majority go to Purgatory, and those who go to Heaven are those from Purgatory. Pray, pray, pray.

My Heart is pierced and full of sorrow. I desire to give my children many graces and peace. They desire to remain in darkness and sin and run after all the desires of the flesh and the world. The world does not hold peace, only death.

Medjugorje

Like the revelations given to Christina Gallagher, the messages and visions concerning Hell given at Medjugorje—the apparition epicenter of the late 20th century—also deserve serious attention. At Medjugorje, the Virgin Mary's plea to the world has been for peace, but on occasion she has spoken in her messages and in private to the six visionaries about Hell, and like at Fatima, showed several of them the abode of the damned.

On November 6, 1981, several of the visionaries were shown Hell. Mary then said to them: "Do not be frightened" I have shown you Hell so that you may know the state of those who are there." Mary would later elaborate on the subject only to emphasize, as she did with Christina Gallagher, that more and more souls are going to Hell. "Today many people go to Hell. God permits His children to suffer in Hell due to the fact that they have committed grave, unpardonable sins. Those who are in Hell no longer have a chance to know a better lot" (1982).

The following year, Mary spoke again of Hell: "The majority of people go to Purgatory, many go to Hell. A small number go directly to Heaven" (1983). In response to a question from a priest about Hell, who asked why God sends souls there, the Virgin replied: "Many who go to

Hell no longer want to receive any benefit from God. They do not repent nor do they cease to revolt and blaspheme. They make up their mind to live in Hell and do not contemplate leaving it." Mary then added that some souls actually start to live in their own personal, living Hell while still on earth.

However, the Virgin's most powerful message at Medjugorje, on Hell came in October 1985: "Those who say "I don't believe in God, how difficult it will be for them when they approach the throne of God and hear the voice: *'Enter into Hell.'*"

★

As at Fatima, the most poignant insights into Hell come from the words of the visionaries who attempt to describe what they saw the day Mary showed them Hell.

Maria Pavlovic Lunetti told Father Renee Laurentin that Hell "was something horrible." The people "suffered and were in pain," said Maria. In her book, *Queen of the Cosmos*, author Janice T. Connoll interviewed Maria about what she saw in Hell:

Q. Marija, have you ever seen Hell?

A. *Yes, it's a large space with a big sea of fire in the middle. There are many people there. I particularly noticed a beautiful young girl. But when she came near the fire, she was not longer beautiful. She came out of the fire like an animal; she was no longer human. The Blessed Mother told me that God gives us all choices. Everyone responds to these choices. Everyone can choose if he wants to go to Hell or not. Anyone who goes to Hell chooses Hell.*

Q. Marija, how and why does a soul choose Hell for himself for all eternity?

A. *In the moment of death, God gives us the light to see ourselves as we really are. God gives freedom of choice to everybody during his life on earth. The one who lives in sin on earth can see what he has done and recognize himself as he really is. When he sees himself and his life, the only possible place for him is Hell. HE chooses Hell, because that is what he is. That is where he fits. It is his own wish. God does not make the choice. God condemns no one. We condemn ourselves. Every individual has free choice. God gave us freedom.*

Q. Marija, what about people who grow up spiritually deceived, people who have been told that God does not exist, that there is no God?

A. *People, as they grow up, can think. Everyone knows and can recognize what is good and what is bad by the time they grow up. God gives us freedom of choice. We can choose good or bad. Everybody chooses here in this life whether he goes to Heaven or Hell.*

Q. How do we choose Heaven or Hell or Purgatory for ourselves, Marija?

A. *At the moment of death, God gives everyone the grace to see his whole life, to see what he has done, to recognize the results of his choices on earth. And each person, when he sees himself in the divine light of reality, chooses for himself what her personally deserves for all eternity.*

★

Like Marija, visionary **Vicka Ivankovic** carries with her lasting memories of the vision of Hell. "In Hell, in the middle, is a huge fire. There are no coals—nothing, just the flames. Many people go, one by one, crying...May God protect us from it!" (Excerpted from *Is the Virgin Mary Appearing at Medjugorje* by Fr. Rene Laurentin and Ljudeult Rupecic.) Hell, Vicka told Janice T. Connell in *Queen of the Cosmos*, was horrible and ugly:

Q. Are Heaven and Hell actual places?

A. *Yes, I saw them.*

Q. How?

A. *Two ways—I saw with my eyes.*

Q. A vision?

A. *Yes, and then I visited these places. Jacov and I were taken there by the Blessed Mother.*

Q. What about Hell—is it a place, too?

A. *Yes.*

Q. Do many people go there today?

A. *Yes. We saw many people in Hell. Many are there already, and many more will go there when they die.*

Q. Why so many?

A. *The Blessed Mother says that those people who are in Hell are there because they chose to go there. They wanted to go to Hell.*

Q. Vicka, why would anyone want to go there?

A. *We all know that there are persons on this earth who simply don't admit that God exists, even though He helps them, gives them life and sun and rain and food. He always tries to nudge them onto the path of holiness. They just say they don't believe, and they deny Him. They deny Him, even when it is time to die. And they continue to deny Him, after they are dead. It is their choice. It is their will that they go to Hell. They choose Hell.*

Q. Describe Hell as you remember it.

A. *In the center of this place is a great fire, like an ocean of raging flames. We could see people before they went into the fire, and then we would see them coming out of the fire. Before they go into the fire, they look like normal people. The more they are against God's will, the deeper they enter into the fire, and the deeper they go, the more they rage against Him. When they come out of the fire, they don't have human shape anymore; they are more like grotesque animals, but unlike anything on earth. It's as if they were never human beings before.*

Q. Can you describe them?

A. *They were horrible. Ugly. Angry. And each was different; no two looked alike.*

Q. After they came out of the ocean of fire, what did they do?

A. *When they came out, they were raging and smashing everything around and hissing and gnashing and screeching.*

Q. Were you afraid?

A. *I am never afraid when I am with the Blessed Mother. But I didn't like seeing this....*

Q. When you were there, could you feel the fire's heat?

A. *No, we were in a special grace with the Blessed Mother, so we felt nothing.*

Q. Vicka, you said that God condemns no one, that people choose Hell for themselves. Would it be fair, then, to say that if you can choose Hell, you can also choose Heaven?

A. *There are two differences: the people on earth who choose Hell know that hey will go there. But nobody is sure on the earth if they are go into Heaven or Purgatory. Not one of us is sure.*

Q. Can you be sure that you are not going to Hell?

A. *Yes. Follow God's will. The most important thing is to know that God loves us.*

Q. How does this knowledge help us to go to Heaven?

A. *When we know for sure that God loves us, we try to love Him in return—to respond to God's love for us by being faithful in good times and bad.*

Q. Has seeing Hell changed how you pray?

A. *Oh, yes! Now I pray for the conversion of sinners! I know what awaits them it they refuse to convert.*

In Connell's second book on Medjugorje, *The Visions of the Children*, Vicka added more to her disclosures:

Q. You described a beautiful young woman who was filled with anger whom you saw enter the fire. You said when she emerged she looked like a type of nonhuman, that she was so ugly you could hardly look. Does that mean that people lose the image and likeness of God that they are born with, as they enter the fire?

A. *Maybe.*

Q. What causes this?

A. *People turn away from God by the choices they make. In this way they choose to enter the fire of hell where they burn away all connection to God. That's why they can never get back to God. It takes God's mercy to get back to Him. In hell, they no longer have access to God's mercy.*

Q. They burn away their personal image and likeness of God by their choices?

A. *Yes. They choose to destroy their beauty and goodness. They choose to be ugly and horrible. People do this all the time. Each choice that is against God, God's commandments, God's will, singes God's image in us.*

Q. Is that why Marija said many people choose hell right here on earth?

A. *Yes, they become one with hell even while they have their body. At death they go on as they were when they had a body.*

Q. Are you saying that we are either God's children or Satan's children?

A. *Yes. We are either for God and with God and in God, or we are victims of Satan. We choose to be one with him.*

Q. Isn't there any middle ground?

A. *No.*

Q. What about people who sin?

A. *We all sin. That's why the Blessed Mother calls us to reconciliation with God and our brothers and sisters now. The more we rebel against God's ways, the farther we are from God's kingdom.*

Q. How do we get back?

A. *As long as we live on earth, we can always get back to God by sorrow for our sins.*

★

Unlike Marija and Vicka, the remaining visionaries at Medjugorje chose either not to see Hell (Ivanka Ivankovic Elez and Mirjana Dragecivic Soldo) or wished not to elaborate on the grim site they beheld. Said Ivan Ivankovic about Hell: "I prefer not to discuss it."

Jacov Colo, the youngest of the visionaries, commented on his experiences, but preferred to limit his response to only the positive. "I choose not to think about Hell," he told Connell, "The self-chosen suffering there is beyond your ability to comprehend....No one needs to go to Hell. It is the ultimate waste!" (From *The Visions of the Children*).

In summation, the visionaries of Medjugorje emphasize the following:

- God sends no one to Hell. People choose Hell by their own choices in life and at their judgment.
- The Virgin Mary has come now, with great urgency, to save souls from Hell.

Salvation! Salvation is the word used over and over again by all who understand why Christ came into the world and why, during our times, Mary is appearing all over the world. We are at a crossroad in history. A great change is about to take place in the world by the hand and will of God. This change, Mary tells visionaries, will be sudden and shocking for many people in the world. If not prepared for what is to come, many will lose their souls, many will go to Hell, the Virgin repeats. This tragedy, the visionaries at Medjugorje emphasize, is not what God wants. God desires, the Virgin Mary repeats over and over, "to save all souls." Perhaps the words of Vicka Ivankovic best summarize Mary's pleas to the world during our time:

> Our Lady wants everyone in the whole world to be saved, to live in God's loving presence. She has come to call all people in the world to listen to her messages and convert. It is dangerous to live in sin. Terrible catastrophes await those who do not turn back to God. But He always forgives us, no matter what sin. All we have to do is ask. The Blessed Mother is calling us to ask His forgiveness now. She reminds us that God never refuses forgiveness to any of His children who ask. ...
>
> It is because everybody is her child. The Blessed Mother says: "*I love everybody as my own son and daughter, and I want everyone to be saved. I don't want a single one of my children in Hell.*" She is hoping people will accept these messages little by little. And they are. She says praying the rosary, especially as a family, and fasting, are powerful ways to rescue souls for the kingdom of her Son. She recommends to us to pray all three mysteries of the rosary every day, the Joyful, Sorrowful and The Glorious. To fast on bread and water every Friday and if possible on Wednesdays, too. When she asks us to pray, she does not mean to pray with mere words; she wants us to pray with our hearts, so that prayer can become a wellspring of happiness of us. Then we will know of God's immense love, of His great mercy. He loves all His children. He forgives; He never turns anyone away, no matter what we have done. (From *Queen of the Cosmos* by Janice T. Connell)

HELL, ME?

It is mortal sin, the Catholic Church teaches, that sends a soul — unrepentant before death—to Hell. Thomas A. Nelson, in his book *How to Avoid Hell*, examines the sins that send a soul to Hell:

> When speaking of mortal and venial sin, the Catholic Church is very careful not to make definite pronouncements on most types of sin as to whether they are mortal or venial because the seriousness of sins can vary, based upon either the circumstances surrounding the sin or the person s awareness of the degree of its sinfulness. These two factors can change so dramatically that in some cases there is a mortal sin, in others there is a venial sin, and in still others there is no sin at all. For example, a poor person with many children to feed may over a period of time may steal a substantial amount of food from a truck farmer because it is the only place near enough from which to obtain food and because the owner will not give it to him; the alternative would be the possible sickness or death of his children. In this case there would probably not even be so much as a slight venial sin, though the person would be duty-bound to pay for the food taken if he ever could.
>
> But the Church *does say* that with regard to some sins the matter is *always* mortally sinful. These sins include sins directly against God (against the First Commandment) and the sins of impurity (against the

Sixth and Ninth Commandments). The Church does
teach that, so long as the three determining factors for
mortal sin are present—namely, 1) a serious matter (or
a matter considered to be serious by the sinner), 2)
sufficient reflection and 3) full consent of the will—then
sins against God (blasphemy, rejecting the gift of Faith,
or purposely not becoming a Catholic when one knows
this is what God wants of all people, apostasy, heresy,
agnosticism, schism) and all sins of impurity...are in
themselves *always* mortally sinful, as are willful murder,
suicide, abortion, artificial birth control, and operations
intended to cause sterility (e.g., tubal ligation,
vasectomy). Such sins are always mortally sinful, given
the presence of the other two factors needed to
constitute a mortal sin.

Other sins can be mortal sins at some times and
venial sins at other times, or no sin at all, depending on
the circumstances. A good example would be lying. If
the lie involves a serious matter, it would be mortally
sinful; if it does not, it would be venially sinful; if the
person asking has no right to know, it would be no sin
at all, but rather, what is called a *mental reservation*.

With this in mind, we can better understand why Christians are
taught to note well the Ten Commandments. The Catholic Catechism
also teaches that the faithful must be on guard against the Seven Capital
Sins: Pride, covetousness, lust, anger, gluttony, envy, and sloth. These
are not sins themselves, unless deliberately consented to. Rather, it is
the conditions or inclinations within us from which sin arises. Let us
examine each:

Pride

Pride is the first Capital Sin because it is the
cause of all sin. This sin denies God and that everything
comes from God. Pride is a sin by which a person
esteems himself. It is inordinate self love. It is the sin of
the fallen angels.

Pride affects our intellect and blinds us to the

truth of matters. The manifestations of pride are self-centeredness, self-pity, conceit, disobedience, indignation, haughtiness, over-ambition, and manipulation and criticism of others.

It is only, theologians say, by the practice of humility that one overcomes pride. A person needs to pray, be patient, act kind, be charitable, practice meekness and submission, along with modesty and sympathy. In essence, we must abandon ourselves more and more to God.

Covetousness

Covetousness is an inordinate love of worldly goods and material possessions. Covetous people are not sympathetic to the poor and basically do not trust in God's providence. To defend against this sin, one must practice generosity, mercy, and trust in God.

Lust

Lust is the desire of the flesh for pleasure, especially sexual pleasure. Outside of marriage, there is no morally acceptable expression of human sexuality. Whether it is in thought, word, or action, lust is impurity. Sins of lust of the mind, of the eyes, even within marriage, are warned about in Scripture. This sin is considered by great theologians and the Doctors of the Church to cause the most loss of souls. The Virgin Mary said so much at Fatima. Modesty of dress, of the eyes, of speech, and of listening combats lust. Complete avoidance of impure attractions and prayer, of course, helps to fight this temptation.

Anger

Anger is an excessive desire to suppress or to respond to that which one perceives to be hostile to oneself. Real or imagined anger, when displayed, is often a passion that leads to further action and often generates a sinful response from others. The sin of anger, when not controlled, can lead to greater sin and to sin by others, especially hatred and violence. Calmness, humility and acceptance of God's will help us to combat anger. The practice of peace is called for in all anger-producing situations. Prayer controls anger.

Envy

Envy is a tendency to begrudge the success of others. From it can come anger, calumny, persecution, and jealousy. Envy is a sin against charity. Envy is a blindness to the actions of God in other's lives or our own. We must trust God to protect us from envy and to develop the habit of seeing and wanting good for others.

Gluttony

Gluttony is the inordinate desire to eat and drink for sheer pleasure. Gluttony is a very easy sin to fall into and often persists in hidden forms. Pleasure from eating and drinking dominates one's behavior causing other sins such as anger and impurity. To control gluttony, we must realize the pleasures in eating and drinking are not ends in themselves. We must strive for temperance, through prayer and fasting.

Sloth

Sloth is laziness, either spiritual or bodily. Sloth can involve apathy, laziness, and basic indifference. Sloth can also hide behind activity that, although considerable, is not what we should be doing. The sin of sloth involves a lack of enthusiasm for growth and development and, perhaps, an undue love of pleasure. To combat sloth, we must be faithful to our duties in life, watch our leisure time, and pray.

★

The Seven Capital Sins are the seven roots of all sin. They are weaknesses and predispose us to evil, especially to mortal sins.

According to the Virgin Mary's revelations, the world is drowning in mortal sin rising from the Seven Capital sins.

But it is especially sins of the flesh, sins of lust, that she says are innumerable in our world today. At Fatima, Mary said that sins of the flesh are what cause "the most souls to go to Hell." This great loss of purity, which violates the 6th and 9th commandments, is pushing the world closer to the edge of disaster. In a message to Father Stefano Gobbi titled, *The Angel of The First Plague*, the Virgin Mary outlined the depth of this reality:

> You are recalling today my last apparition, which took place at Fatima on the 13th of October, 1917, confirmed by the miracle of the sun. Look more and more to the Woman Clothed with the Sun, who has the task of preparing the Church and humanity for the coming of the great Day of the Lord.
>
> The times of the decisive battle have come. The hour of the great tribulation has now descended upon the world, because the angels of the Lord are being sent, with their plagues, to chastise the earth.
>
> How many times have I urged you to walk along the road of mortification of the senses, of mastery over the passions, of modesty, of good example, of purity and of holiness! But humanity has not accepted my urging and has continued to disobey the sixth commandment of the law of the Lord which prescribes that one shall not commit impure acts.
>
> On the contrary, it has sought to exalt such a transgression and to put it forward as the acquisition of a human value and a new way of exercising one's own personal freedom. Thus, today it has reached the point of legitimating as good all the sins of impurity. It has begun to corrupt the consciences of little children and of youth, bringing them to the conviction that impure acts committed by oneself are no longer sins; that relations before marriage between those engaged is licit and good; that families may behave as they please and may also make use of the various means of birth control.

And they have come to the justification and the exaltation of impure acts against nature and even to the proposing laws which put homosexual cohabitation on a par with marriage.

Never as today have immorality, impurity, and obscenity been so continually propagandized through the press and all the means of social communication. Above all, television has become the perverse instrument of a daily bombardment with obscene images, directed to corrupt the purity of the mind and the heart of all. The places of entertainment—in particular the cinema and the discotheques—have become places of public profanation of one's human and Christian dignity.

This is the time when the Lord our God is being continually and publicly offended by sins of the flesh. Holy Scripture has already warned you that those who sin by means of the flesh find their just punishment in that same flesh. And so the time has come when *the Angel of the first plague* is passing over the world, that it might be chastised according to the will of God.

The Angel of the first plague cuts into the flesh of those who have allowed themselves to be signed with the mark of the monster on the forehead and on the hand and have adored his image *with a painful and malignant wound*, which causes those who have been stricken by it to cry out in desperation. This wound represents the physical pain which strikes the body by means of grave and incurable maladies. The painful and malignant wound is a plague for all humanity, today so perverted, which has built up an atheistic and materialistic civilization and has made the quest for pleasure the supreme aim of human life. Some of my poor children have been stricken by it because of their sins of impurity and their disordered morals and they carry within their own selves the weight of the evil they have done. Others, on the other hand, have been stricken, even though they are good and innocent; and so their suffering serves for the salvation of many of the wicked, in virtue of the solidarity which unites you all.

The first plague is that of malignant tumors and every kind of cancer, against which science can do nothing notwithstanding its progress in every field, maladies which spread more and more and strike the human body, devastating it with most painful and malignant wounds. Beloved children, think of the spread of these incurable maladies, throughout every part of the world, and of the millions of deaths which they are bringing about.

The first plague is the new malady of AIDS, which strikes above all my poor children who are victims of drugs, of vices, and of impure sins against nature.

Your heavenly Mother wants to be a help, a support, a comfort and a source of hope for all in these times when humanity is being stricken by this first plague. For this, I urge you all to walk along the road of fasting, of mortification, and of penance.

Of little children I ask that they grow in the virtue of purity and, in this difficult journey, let them be assisted by their parents and teachers.

Of *the youth* I ask that they form themselves in the control of the passions through prayer and a life a union with me, and that they renounce going to the cinema and the discotheques, were there exists the grave and continuous danger of offending this virtue which is so dear to my Immaculate Heart.

Of *engaged couples* I ask that they abstain from all relations before marriage.

Of *Christian husbands and wives* I ask that they form themselves in the exercise of conjugal chastity and never make use of artificial means of birth control, as they follow the teaching of Christ, which the Church still puts forth today with enlightened wisdom.

How very must I ask *of priests* the scrupulous observance of celibacy, and *of religious*, the faithful and austere practice of their vow of chastity!

To my poor children, stricken by the first plague of the painful and malignant wound, I present myself as a merciful Mother, who assuages and comforts, who brings to hope and to peace. Of these I ask that they offer their sufferings in a spirit of reparation, of purification and of sanctification. Above all, for them my Immaculate Heart becomes the most welcome refuge and the sure road that leads them to the God of salvation and of joy.

In this, my heavenly garden, all will be consoled and encouraged, while I myself personally and lovingly take care to give consolation in suffering and, if it be in the will of the Lord, to offer the gift of healing.

Consequently, in this time when humanity is being stricken by the first plague, I urge you all to look to me, your heavenly Mother, that you may be comforted and assisted. (October 13, 1989)

★

Sin, especially mortal sin, is destroying humanity. But such a fate is not only true for individuals, Mary says, but also for nations. Indeed, Scripture speaks of the effect of sin on nations, too, and how this leads to the "death of nations." Nations, then, like individual souls, will be judged. This truth has not been fully understood during our times. Times in which individual freedom is glorified and desired more than the greater good. Times in which we downplay the consequences of sin, rationalizing that the effects of sin only involve the individual sinner.

But God makes it clear in Scripture that the sins of individuals affect us all. Therefore, judgement will come to the nations, Scripture says, and nations will be condemned.

What, therefore, can we do? Scripture teaches that we must pray, we must be vigilant, and we must truly repent for our sins—individually and collectively. For without such actions we will have no recourse on Judgment Day. Perhaps the words of Thomas A. Nelson, from his book *How To Avoid Hell*, can serve as an inspiration for us individually, for our nation, and for our world and as we come to the realization that the Day of the Lord is coming:

We all know with our natural reason, unaided by Revelation, that there is an afterlife. We all know (however deeply and inchoately within ourselves it may be) that a final reckoning is coming at the end of our lives, a Day of Judgement, when all will be put right and when final justice, will be done. We know, too, within our heart of hearts, that our own eternal destiny will be determined by how we live and what we do here in this world. We all know that when we commit mortal sin, we must either accept the fact we are thereby on the road to Hell, or we have to lie to ourselves and say, "It isn't a sin." Or, "It isn't that bad." Or, "But God understands. He will have mercy."

Yes, He does indeed understand, and He surely will have mercy *on the truly repentant* (otherwise, who among us would ever be saved); but He is also just, in fact He is Justice Itself, and it is His very justice that will condemn us if we do not repent of our mortal sins—all of them—and if we do not do penance and amend our lives once and for all before we die.

People wait and wait while they live on and on in the state of mortal sin, thinking always within themselves: "I must change. I must correct my life.....soon!" But for many mortal sinners "soon" never comes, as months drift into years, and as they continue to defer the time of their conversion—many until it is too late—and they are cut off by an accident or a heart attack while still at the fullness of their powers, or until they have grown old and become sick or senile and have not the mental strength anymore to focus on the eternal questions of Heaven or Hell and just what God requires us to do to satisfy His justice in order to be saved.

But the certain way to avoid Hell is to start *now*, from wherever we might be, and turn to God, asking of Him the gift of Faith, true repentance, the forgiveness of our sins, a spirit of penance (to make up to Him for our lost years spent in sin and self-indulgence) and the virtue of charity—a Godlike love of God and of our fellow man. If we are Catholic, we must go to Confession with the proper dispositions—at least of imperfect contrition for all the mortal sins we may have committed and with a firm resolve to commit mortal sin no more. And if we are not Catholic, we should approach the Catholic Church, which is none other than Christ Himself extended in time and presented to the world.

At that point we shall THEN have entered upon the field of battle and THEN we can begin in earnest the job of our salvation. "Stand, therefore, having your loins girt about with truth, and having on the breastplate of justice, and your feet shod with the preparation of the gospel of peace: In all things taking the shield of faith, wherewith you may be able to extinguish all the fiery darts of the most wicked one (Eph 6:14-16).

It is not until we become truly Catholic that we *begin* to live the life of Christ here in this world, that we *begin* to prepare ourselves for Heaven by living a life of virtue—a life wherein we start to observe meticulously all the Commandments, root our the Seven Capital Sins, practice virtue seriously, pray, receive the Sacraments instituted by Christ to help us with His grace, live a life of true Christian charity, and start on the road to being as "perfect as our Heavenly Father is perfect" (Mt 5:48).

NOTES

PART I — INSIDE HEAVEN

CHAPTER ONE
LOOKING FOR HEAVEN

The information on the anthropological discoveries in China and Iraq comes from *Quest For the Past*, pgs 48-49, published by Reader's Digest. Further historical facts concerning ancient Mesopotamian burial practices were drawn from *The Universal Standard Encyclopedia* (1956). The information on the early Semite practices came from *Heaven: A History*, by Colleen McDannell and Bernhard Lang, pg 3. The quotation is from page 6 of the same book. For a very thorough, scholarly treatment of the subject of Heaven, I highly recommend this book. It is published by Yale University Press (1988) and available in most bookstores.

The primary source for the ancient Greek concept of Heaven is McDannell and Lang's book, *Heaven: a History* and *A History of Heaven*, by Jeffrey Burton Russell. Russell's book is also highly recommended and was featured in a **Newsweek** magazine article on Heaven in 1997. It is published by Princeton University Press (1997) and available in most bookstores. The comparison between the Greek and Hebrew concepts of Heaven at the end of the chapter was influenced by Peter Kreeft's analysis in his book *Heaven, the Heart's Deepest Longing*, Ignatius Press, San Francisco, 1989. Perhaps no contemporary Catholic writer does this subject as much justice as Kreeft. I believe he has written other books on the afterlife.

CHAPTER TWO
THE PROMISED LAND

Peter Kreeft's quotation is from pages 14, 15, & 16 of his book *Heaven the Heart's Deepest Longing*. Once more, this book is highly recommended. Much of the information on Sheol comes from Russell's *A History of Heaven* and McDannell and Lang's book *Heaven: a History*. The reference themes from the Old Testament are take from *A Textual Concordance of Holy Scripture* by Fr. Thomas David Williams (TAN Books), first published in 1908. Jeffrey Burton Russell's quotation is from page 33 of his book. Russell's and McDannell and Lang's books both contribute greatly to the historic outline presented at the end of this chapter.

CHAPTER THREE
INHERITING THE KINGDOM

Christ's teachings on Heaven are primarily drawn from *A Textual Concordance of Holy Scripture* (TAN Books) by Fr. Thomas David Williams. The Scriptural passages are from *The New American Bible*, Catholic Bible Publishers, Wichita; Kansas. (1984-85 edition).

CHAPTER FOUR
THE NEW JERUSALEM

The Jeffrey Burton Russell quotation is from his book *A History of Heaven*, pgs. 50-52.

CHAPTER FIVE
THE COMMUNION OF SAINTS

The Jeffrey Burton Russell quotations are from his book *A History of Heaven*, pgs, 55, 106-108. Russell's research on the vision literature of the Middle Ages is excellent and recommended reading. The McDannell and Lang quotation is from their book *Heaven A History*, pg.109. The *Catechism of the Council of Trent* and *1994 Catechism of the Catholic Church* texts are listed in the bibliography.

CHAPTERS SIX
VISIONS OF HEAVEN

The account of St. Saturus and St. Perpetua is from *Butler's Lives of the Saints*. The story of the soldier's vision according to St. Gregory's *Dialogue* came from Russell's book *A History of Heaven*, pg. 98. The story of St. Dominic is from Augusta Theodosia Drane's book, *The Life of St. Dominic*, Tan Books 1988. The account of St. Birgitta of Sweden comes from the book *Birgitta of Sweden*, published by Paulist Press (1990), pgs 102-103. This book I highly recommend. The account of St. Rita is from the book *St. Rita of Cascia*, by Fr. Joseph Sicardo, O.S.A., TAN Books. The account of Julianna of Norwich comes from the book *Revelations of the Divine Love, Julianna of Norwich*, published by Image Books, 1977. The account of Heaven from Mary of Agreda is from her classic, *Mystical City of God*, published by TAN Books. The account from the Venerable Anne Catherine Emmerich is from *The Life of Anne Catherine Emmerich, Volumes 1-2*, TAN Books. St. Don Bosco's dream of Heaven comes from *Dreams, Visions and Prophecies of Don Bosco*, edited by Reverend Eugene Brown, Don Bosco Publications, New Rochelle, New York (1986). This book I highly recommend.

CHAPTER SEVEN
THE QUEEN OF HEAVEN

The revelations of Sister Faustina Kowalska come from the book *Divine Mercy in My Soul — The Diary of Sister M. Faustina Kowalska*. This book is available through the Marian Press, Stockbridge, Massachusetts.

The experiences of Christina Gallagher are from the author's book, *The Sorrow, The Sacrifice and the Triumph — The Apparitions, Visions and Prophecies of Christina Gallagher* (Simon and Schuster). The story of Georgette Faniel comes from the author's book, *Glory To The Father, A Brief Look at the Mystical Life of Georgette Faniel.* (St. Andrew's Productions) All of Father Stefano Gobbi's revelations come from the Marian Movement of Priest's book, *To The Priests, Our Lady's Beloved Sons*, and are used with permission.

The interviews with the visionaries of Medjugorje come from Janice T. Connell's two books on Medjugorje, *Queen of the Cosmos* (Paraclete Press, 1990) and *The Visions of the Children*, (St. Martin's Press, 1992). Both of these books are unparalleled in their clarity of the message of Medjugorje and are highly recommended. I also used Fr. Ljudevit Rupcic's and Father Réne Laurentin's book, *Is the Virgin Mary Appearing in Medjugorje?* (The Word Among Us Press, 1984).

CHAPTER EIGHT
THE BEATIFIC VISION

Fr. Garrigou Lagrange's quotations came from his book, *Everlasting Life*, (TAN Books). I used this book as a general reference book on the theology of Heaven. It is highly recommended.

NOTES

PART II — INSIDE HELL

CHAPTER NINE
THE NEED FOR JUSTICE

I used many references to attempt to piece together some of the early "history of Hell". I especially recommend Alice Turner's *The History of Hell* (Harcourt Brace and Company, 1993), and Charles Panati's *Sacred Origins of Profound Things* (Penguin Group, 1996). Fr. Garrigou Lagrange's quotation is from his book, *Life Everlasting, pgs. 99-100,* (TAN Books). St. Alphonsus Liguori's quotations on Hell are from his book, *What Will Hell be Like? pgs. 1-5, 7-8,* (TAN Books). St. Robert Bellarmine's quotation is from his book, *Hell and It's Torments,* pgs. 42, 43, (TAN Books).

CHAPTER TEN
THE FIRES OF GEHENNA

Scripture references were taken from *The New American Bible,* Catholic Bible Publishers, Wichita; Kansas (1984-85 edition). In this chapter, I referenced many books, but especially I again note Fr. Lagrange's work as well as Sts. Alphonsus and Bellarmine (see Notes-Chapter One). I primarily used Fr. Thomas David William's *A Textual Concordance of the Holy Scripture* (TAN Books), to assemble the specific scriptural teachings on Hell.

CHAPTER ELEVEN
AN UNQUENCHABLE FIRE

I used *Image Book's* version of St. Augustine's *City of God* for the St. Augustine's quotations. This is an excellent pocket size book available in most Catholic bookstores (Double Day Co. Inc., Garden City, New York.) *The Catechism of the Council Trent* is available from TAN Books. I used Urbi Et. Orbi's *Catechism of the Catholic Church,* available through **Inside the Vatican.**

CHAPTER TWELVE
I AM IN HERE FOR ALL ETERNITY

I used and highly recommend Alice Turner's *History of Hell* for some of the research material in this chapter. Fr. F.X. Schouppe's book, *Hell* is a controversial classic, but a must read. It is available from TAN Books. The short accounts of visitations from souls condemned to Hell in this chapter were all taken from Fr. Schouppe's book (see pages 1-100). St. Teresa's of Avila experience with Hell is from her *Autobiography.*

CHAPTER THIRTEEN
HELL UNLEASHED

The revelations of Hell of the Venerable Anne Catherine Emmerich were quoted from *The Life of Jesus Christ and Biblical Revelations* by Ven. Anne Catherine Emmerich, Volume 4, pgs. 354-356, (TAN Books). St. Don Bosco's dream, To Hell and Back is from *Dreams, Visions and Prophecies of Don Bosco*, published by Don Bosco Publications. New Rochelle, New York. This book is highly recommended.

CHAPTER FOURTEEN
GOD WANTS TO SAVE SOULS

Fr. Lamy's quotation is from the book *Pére Lamy, pg. 104,* by Comte Paul Biver (TAN Books). Sister Lucia Santo's memoirs (1 through 4) are from the book *Fatima: In Lucia's Own Words* (Postulation Centre, Fatima, Portugal). Sr. Josefa Menedez's account of her trip to Hell is from her book, *The Way of Divine Love,* by Sister Josefa Menedez (TAN Books, pgs. 143-146). Sister Faustina Kowalska's account of Hell is from her book *Divine Mercy in My Soul, The Diary of Sister Faustina Kowalska* (Diary number 741), pages 296-297. This book is a classic and can be obtained from Marian Press, Stockbridge, Mass. Christina Gallagher's revelations of Hell are from the author's book, *The Sorrow, the Sacrifice and the Triumph - The Apparitions, Visions and Prophecies of Christina Gallagher* (Simon and Schuster, 1995).

The Medjugorje revelations of Hell are primarily from Janice T. Connell's two exceptional works, *Queen of the Cosmos* (Paraclete Press) and *The Visions of the Children* (St. Martin). Both of these books are perhaps as good as any ever published on Medjugorje. *The Visions of the Children* was released in a revised edition in 1998 and is available in almost all bookstores. I also referenced Fr. Ljudevit Rupcic's and Fr. Rene Laurentin's first book on Medjugorje, *Is the Virgin Mary Appearing in Medjugorje?* (Word Among Us Press, Washington, Dec. 1984.) Vicka Ivankovic's plea to the world for conversion is from Janice T. Connell's *Queen of the Cosmos* (Paraclete Press, 1990, pgs. 51 and 57.)

EPILOGUE
HELL, ME?

Thomas A. Nelson's writings on the sins that send a soul to Hell are from the book, *Hell and How to Avoid Hell* (TAN Books). This work is a masterpiece, a book every Catholic should read. It is highly recommended. The Seven Capital Sins can be found in any book on Catholic doctrine. The Virgin Mary's message to Father Stefano Gobbi is from the book, *To the Priests, Our Lady's Beloved Sons,* published by the Marian Movement of Priests. It is used with permission.

SELECTED BIBLIOGRAPHY

A Friend of Medjugorje. *Words from Heaven*. Sterrett, Alabama: Caritas of Birmingham (Published with permission from St. James Publishing), 1996.

Arnendzen, J.P., D.D. *Purgatory and Heaven*. TAN Books and Publishers, Inc., 1972.

Augustine, Saint. *St. Augustine - City of God*. Garden City, New York: Image Books-Doubleday & Company, Inc., 1958.

Bellarmine, St. Robert. *Hell and It's Torments*. Rockford, Illinois: TAN Books and Publishers, Inc., 1990.

Bessieres, Albert, S.J. *Wife, Mother and Mystic* (Blessed Anna Marie Taigi). Rockford, Illinois: TAN Books and Publishers, Inc., 1970.

Biver, Comte Paul, *Père Lamy*. Rockford, Illinois: TAN Books and publishers, Inc., 1973.

Boudreau, Fr. J., S.J. *The Happiness of Heaven*. Rockford, Illinois: TAN Books and Publishers, Inc., 1984.

Broderick, Robert C. *Heaven, The Undiscovered Country*. Huntingdon, Indiana: Our Sunday Visitor, Inc., 1990.

Brown, Rev. Eugene (Ed.). *Dreams, Visions & Prophecies of Don Bosco*. New Rochelle, New York: Don Bosco Publications, 1986.

Brown, Michael H. *Afterlife*. Milford, Ohio: Faith Publishing Company, 1997.

Carty, Rev. Charles Mortimer. *Padre Pio, The Stigmatist*. Rockford, Illinois: TAN Books and Publishers, Inc., 1973.

Carty, Fr. Chas. M. & Rev. Dr. David L. Rumble, M.S.C. *Purgatory Quizzess to a Street Preacher*. Rockford, Illinois: TAN Books and Publishers, Inc., 1976.

----. *Catechism of the Catholic Church*. New Hope, Kentucky: St. Martin de Porres Community, 1994.

Chervin, Ronda DeSola. *Quotable Saints*. Ann Arbor, Michigan: Servant Publications, 1992.

Connell, Janice T. *Queen of the Cosmos*. Orleans, Massachusetts: Paraclete Press, 1990.

Connell, Janice T. *The Visions of the Children*. New York: St. Martin's Press, 1992. [Revised edition, 1998]

Criswell, W.A. and Paige Patterson. *Heaven*. Wheaton, Illinois: Tyndale House Publishers, Inc., 1991.

Delaney John J. *Pocket Dictionary of Saints*. New York: Image-Doubleday, 1980.

Dirvin, Father Joseph I., C.M. *Saint Catherine Laboure of the Miraculous Medal.* Rockford, Illinois: TAN Books and Publishers, Inc., 1984.

Drane, Augusta Theodosia. *The Life of Saint Dominic.* Rockford, Illinois: TAN Books and Publishers, Inc., 1988.

Freze, S.F.O. *Voices, Visions and Apparitions.* Huntington, Indiana: Our Sunday Visitor Publishing Division, 1993.

Gobbi, Don Stefano. *Our Lady Speaks to Her Beloved Priests.* St. Francis, Maine: National Headquarters of the Marian Movement of Priests in the United States of America, 1988.

Gobbi, Don Stefano. *To the Priests Our Lady's Beloved Sons.* St. Francis, Maine: National Headquarters of the Marian Movement of Priests in the United States of America, (Supplement, 1996).

Gouin, Fr. Paul. *Sister Mary of the Cross: Shepherdess of La Salette.* (Printed with permission from The 101 Foundation Asbury, New Jersey: (no date)).

Haffert, John M. *Her Glorious Title Our Lady of Mount Carmel, Star of the Sea.* Asbury, New Jersey: The 101 Foundation, Inc., 1993.

Haffert, John M. *Sign of Her Heart.* Washington, New Jersey: Ave Maria Institute 1971.

Jahenny, Marie-Julie. *Prophecies of La Fraudais.* Monstsurs, France: Editions Resiac, 1977.

Juliana of Norwich. *Revelations of Love.* Garden City, New York: 1977.

Klein, Rev. Peter. *Catholic Source Book.* Worthington, Minnesota: The Printers, 1980.

Kondor, Fr. Louis S.V.D. (Ed.) *Fatima in Lucia's Own Words.* Still River Massachusetts: Marian Helpers, 1991.

Kreeft, Peter, *Heaven, the Heart's Deepest Longing.* San Francisco, California: Ignatius Press, 1989.

Lagrange, Garrigou, Fr. Reginald, O.P. *Everlasting Life.* Rockford, Illinois: TAN Books and Publishers, Inc., 1991.

Laurentin, Rene and Ljudevit Rupcic. *Is the Virgin Mary Appearing at Medjugorje?* Washington, D.C.: The Word Among Us Press, 1984.

Laux, Fr. John, M.A. *Church History.* Rockford, Illinois: TAN Books and Publishers Inc., 1989.

Laux, Fr. John, M.A. *Chief Truths of the Faith. A Course in Religion Book I.* Rockford, Illinois: TAN Books and Publishers, Inc., 1990.

Lord, Bob & Penny, *Visions of Heaven Hell and Purgatory.* Robert and Penny Lord, 1996.

Liguori, St. Alphonsus, *Preparation for Death.* Rockford, Illinois: TAN Books and Publishers, Inc., 1982.

Manning, Henry Edward. *Sin and Its Consequences.* Rockford, Illinois: TAN Books and Publishers, Inc., 1986.

Martin, Regis. *The Hope and Reality of Heaven.* Steubenville, Ohio: Franciscan University Press, 1993.

McDannell, Colleen & Bernhard Lang, *Heaven A History.* New Haven and London: Yale University Press., 1988.

McGeady, Sister Mary Rose. *"Am I Going to Heaven?"* United States of America: Covenant House, 1994.

McGinn, Bernard, et. al., (Ed.) *Birgitta of Sweden.* New York: Paulist Press, 1990.

Menendez, Sister Josefa. *The Way of Divine Love.* Rockford, Illinois: TAN Books and Publishers, Inc., 1972.

Morse, Joseph Laffan, Sc.B., LL.B., LL.D. (Ed.) *The Universal Standard Encyclopedia* (Vol. 25). New York: Standard Reference Works Publishing Company, Inc., 1956.

Nageleisen, Rev. John A. *Charity for the Suffering Souls.* Rockford, Illinois: TAN Books and Publishers, Inc., 1982.

New American Bible, The, Catholic Bible Publishers, Wichita; Kansas. (1984-85 edition).

O'Sullivan, Fr. Paul, O.P. (E.D.M.) *How to Avoid Purgatory.* Rockford, Illinois: TAN Books and Publishers, Inc., 1992.

Panati, Charles. *Sacred Origins of Profound Things.* New York, New York: Penguin Books, USA., Inc., 1996.

Parente, Fr. Alessio, O.F.M. Cap. *The Holy Souls "Viva Padre Pio".* Barto, Pennsylvania: National Centre for Padre Pio, Inc., 1990.

Petit, Berthe. *The Sorrowful and Immaculate Heart of Mary.* Kenosha, Wisconsin: The Franciscan Marytown Press, 1966.

Petrisko, Thomas W. *Call of the Ages.* Santa Barbara, California: Queenship Publishing Company, 1996.

Petrisko, Thomas W. *The Fatima Prophecies: At the Doorstep of the World.* McKees Rocks, Pennsylvania: St. Andrew's Productions, 1998.

Petrisko, Thomas W. *The Sorrow, The Sacrifice, and the Triumph: The Apparitions, Visions and Prophecies of Christina Gallagher.* New York: Simon & Schuster, Inc., 1995.

Peyret, Rev. Raymond. *Marthe Robin: The Cross and the Joy.* Staten Island, New York: Alba House, 1983.

Polley, Jane (ed.) *Quest for the Past.* Pleasantville, N.Y.: Reader's Digest Association, Inc., 1984.

Ruffin, C. Bernard. *Padre Pio: The True Story.* Huntingdon, Indiana: Our Sunday Visitor, Inc., 1991.

Russell, Jeffrey Burton. *A History of Heaven.* Princeton, New Jersey: Princeton University Press, 1997.

Schmoger, Very Rev. Carl E., C.SS.R. *The Life of Anne Catherine Emmerich - Volume 1-2.* Rockford, Illinois: TAN Books and Publishers, Inc., 1976.

Schmoger, Very Rev. Carl E., C.SS.R. (ed.) *The Life of Jesus Christ and Biblical Revelations - Vols. 1-4 (From the Visions of the Venerable Anne Catherine Emmerich as Recorded by the Journals of Clemens Brentano)* Rockford, Illinois: TAN Books and Publishers, Inc., 1979.

Schouppe, Fr. S.X., S.J. *Hell.* Rockford, Illinois: TAN Books and Publishers, Inc., 1989.

Schouppe, Fr. F.X., S.J. *Purgatory.* Rockford, Illinois: TAN Books and Publishers, Inc., 1986.

Sicardo, Fr. Joseph, O.S.A. *St. Rita of Cascia.* Rockford, Illinois: TAN Books and Publishers,

Inc., 1990.

Suarez, Federico. *The Afterlife Death, Judgement, Heaven and Hell*. Manila, Phillipapines: Sinag-tala Publishers, Inc., 1986 (English translation).

----. *The Catechism of the Council of Trent*. Rockford, Illinois: TAN Books and Publishers, Inc., 1982,

----. *The Spiritual Doctrine of Saint Catherine of Genoa*. Rockford, Illinois: TAN Books and Publishers, Inc., 1989.

Thurston, Herbert J., S.J. and Donald Attwater (eds.) *Butler's Lives of the Saints - Volume IV*. Allen, Texas: Christian Classics, 1996.

Turner, Alice K. *The History of Hell*. San Diego, California: Harcourt Brace & Company, 1993.

Vogl, Aldabert Albert. *Theresa Neumann Mystic and Stigmatist*. Rockford, Illinois: TAN Books and Publishers, Inc., 1985.

von Cochem, Fr. Martin, O.S.FC. *The Four Last Things - Death Judgment Hell Heaven*. Rockford, Illinois: TAN Books and Publishers, Inc., 1987.

Wales, Sean, C.SS.R. *The Last Things*. Liguori, Missouri: Publications, 1993.

Williams, Fr. Thomas David. *A Textual Concordance of the Holy Scriptures*. Rockford, Illinois: TAN Books and Publishers, Inc.

THE THIRD SECRET OF FATIMA VISION

Special Edition Prints Available!

Prayer Card	$ 1.00	*Includes Shipping*
8 x 10" Print Only	$ 5.00	+ $2.00 S/H
8 x 10" Gold Frame	$26.00	+ $6.00 S/H
12 x 16" Print Only	$ 8.00	+ $4.00 S/H
12 x 16" Gold Frame	$50.00	+ $10.00 S/H

20 x 24" Gicleé Gold Framed Print on 100% cotton paper,
$200 + Call for Shipping/Insurance

TO ORDER CALL: 1-412-787-9735
PLEASE CALL FOR QUANTITY PURCHASES

208

Help Spread the '*Queen of Peace*' Newspaper!

1 copy - $3.00
25 copies - $20.00
50 copies - $36.00
100 copies - $60.00
Over 100 copies - Call
Complete Set - $12.00

TO ORDER CALL - 412-787-9791
Order the *Queen of Peace* Newspapers in Quantity and Save!
Prices Include Shipping and Handling
★ *Newspaper Special* ★
Order the Complete Set for Only $12

Secret of Fatima Edition
This 2001 edition takes a closer look at the Secret of Fatima, and in particular, the 'Third Secret' which was revealed by the Church on June 26, 2000. Included is the commentary written by Cardinal Ratzinger, which accompanied the secret's release.

Afterlife Edition
This edition examines the actual places of Heaven, Hell and Purgatory through the eyes of the Saints, Mystics, Visionaries, and Blessed Mother herself. Will you be ready come judgment day?

Illumination Edition
This edition focuses on a coming 'day of enlightenment' in which every person on earth will see their souls in the same light that God sees them. Commonly referred to as the 'Warning' or 'Mini-Judgment', many saints and visionaries, particularly the Blessed Mother have spoken about this great event, now said to be imminent.

Eternal Father Edition
This edition makes visible the love and tenderness of God the Father and introduces a special consecration to Him. Many of His messages for the world today tell of the great love He has for all of His 'Prodigal Children.'

Holy Spirit Edition
This edition reveals how the Holy Spirit continues to work through time and history, raising up great saints in the Church. Emphasized in the hidden, yet important role of St. Joseph.

Eucharistic Edition
This edition contains evidence for the Real Presence of Christ in the Eucharist. Many miracles and messages are recorded to reaffirm this truth.

Special Edition III
This edition focuses on the great prophecies the Blessed Mother has given to the world since her apparitions in 1917 at Fatima. Prophetic events related to the 'Triumph of Her Immaculate Heart' are addressed in detail.

Special Edition II
This edition examines the apparitions of the Blessed Mother at Fatima and in relation to today's apparitions occurring worldwide.

Special Edition I
The first in a trilogy of the apparitions and messages of the Blessed Mother, this edition tells why Mary has come to earth and is appearing to all parts of the world today.

Best Sellers by Dr. Thomas W. Petrisko!

Inside Purgatory

What History, Theology, and the Mystics tell us about Purgatory
The follow up book to the best-seller '*Inside Heaven and Hell*'
this books continues on in the same 'reader-friendly' format.
Guiding the reader through the teachings of the Church and
Scripture, this book is also enhanced by what mystics, visionaries,
saints and scholars tell us about this mysterious place. **$10.95**

The Miracle of the Illumination of All Consciences

Known as the 'Warning' or 'Mini-Judgment' a coming "day of
enlightenment" has been foretold. It is purported to be a day
in which God will supernaturally illuminate the conscience
of every man, woman, and child on earth. Each person, then,
would momentarily see the state of their soul through God's
eyes and realize the truth of His existence. **$12.95**

The Fatima Prophecies

At the Doorstep of the World
This powerhouse book tells of the many contemporary
prophecies and apparitions and how they point to the
fulfillment of Fatima's two remaining prophecies, the
'annihilation of nations' and 'era of peace'. Is the world about
to enter the era of peace or will there be a terrible
chastisement? Contains over 60 pictures. **$16.95**

Fatima's Third Secret Explained

Officially made public to the world on June 26, 2000, the
controversial *Third Secret* of Fatima is not easily understood. This
work seeks to explain the *Third Secret* in the context of the
entire message of Fatima and decipher what it might mean for
the world today. Included is the invaluable commentary written
by Cardinal Ratzinger which accompanied the secrets release.
The book also contains a photocopy of the original *Third
Secret* text written in Sr. Lucia's own handwriting. **$12.95**

Toll-Free (888) 654-6279 or (412) 787-9735 www.SaintAndrew.com

St. Andrew's Productions Order Form

Order Toll-Free! 1-888-654-6279 or 1-412-787-9735
Visa, MasterCard Accepted!

_____	Call of the Ages (Petrisko)	$12.95
_____	Catholic Answers for Catholic Parents	$ 8.95
_____	Catholic Parents Internet Guide	$ 3.00
_____	Face of the Father, The (Petrisko)	$ 9.95
_____	False Prophets of Today (Petrisko)	$ 7.95
_____	Fatima Prophecies, The (Petrisko)	$14.95
_____	Fatima's Third Secret Explained (Petrisko)	$14.99
_____	Finding Our Father (Centilli)	$ 4.95
_____	Glory to the Father (Petrisko)	$ 8.95
_____	God 2000 (Fr. Richard Foley, SJ)	$11.95
_____	Holy Spirit in the Writings of PJP II	$19.95
_____	In God's Hands (Petrisko)	$12.95
_____	Inside Heaven and Hell (Petrisko)	$14.95
_____	Inside Purgatory (Petrisko)	$10.95
_____	Kingdom of Our Father, The (Petrisko)	$16.95
_____	Last Crusade, The (Petrisko)	$ 9.95
_____	Mary in the Church Today (McCarthy)	$14.95
_____	Miracle of the Illumination, The	$12.95
_____	Prophecy of Daniel, The (Petrisko)	$ 7.95
_____	Prodigal Children, The (Centilli)	$ 4.95
_____	Seeing with the Eyes of the Soul: Vol. 1	$ 3.00
_____	Seeing with the Eyes of the Soul: Vol. 2	$ 3.00
_____	Seeing with the Eyes of the Soul: Vol. 3	$ 3.00
_____	Seeing with the Eyes of the Soul: Vol. 4	$ 3.00
_____	Sorrow, Sacrifice and the Triumph	$13.00
_____	St. Joseph and the Triumph (Petrisko)	$10.95

Queen of Peace Newspapers
_____ *Afterlife Edition* (Heaven, Hell and Purgatory) $3.00ea.

Name:_____

Address:_____

City:_____St____Zip_____

Phone:_____Fax_____

Visa/MasterCard_____

Total Enclosed:_____

PLEASE ADD SHIPPING/TAX
$0-24.99...$4.00, $25-49.99...$6.00, $50-99.99...$8.00, $100 + Add 8%
PA Residents Add 7% Tax
OR MAIL ORDER TO:
St. Andrew's Productions, 6111 Steubenville Pike, McKees Rocks, PA   15136
www.SaintAndrew.com

Printed in the United States
44183LVS00007B/208-216